Some Assembly Required

How to Make, Grow and Keep
Your Business Relationships

S e c o n d   E d i t i o n

Thom Singer
with Leslie Morris

Ed—
Never Stop
Networking!!!

New Year Publishing, LLC

Danville, California

Thom Singer

Some Assembly Required:

How to Make, Grow and Keep
Your Business Relationships

S e c o n d   E d i t i o n

by Thom Singer with Leslie Morris

Published by:
New Year Publishing, LLC
144 Diablo Ranch Ct.
Danville, CA 94506 USA

http://www.newyearpublishing.com

Design by: Your Art Director, www.yourartdirector.com

Library of Congress Control Number: 2007930311

ISBN: 978-0-9760095-3-5

Contents

To my wife, Sara. Without you, nothing in my life would be complete. I enjoy the journey of our marriage and the real adventure of raising our children. Thank you for your love and support on this book, and on all that I do.

To my daughters, Jackie and Kate. There is no gift in this world as special as Daddy's Little Girl and I am blessed to have two of you! Watching you both grow up and discover the world is an amazing experience. You are delightful.

To my parents, Al and Betty Singer. I cannot find the words to properly say thank you. I love you and appreciate all you both have taught me. Even though you are no longer with us, Mom, you still continue to influence me. Dad, you inspire me by the life you live. You have the greatest outlook of anyone I have ever met and I hope that I can be half as good of a father to my children.

ACKNOWLEDGEMENTS

The creation of this book has truly been an amazing process. While I have wanted to write a book for more than 20 years, it was not until now that the stars were aligned and I was able to tackle the project. I believe strongly that relationships with other people make us stronger than we could be on our own, and I hope that this comes through on these pages.

Like any accomplishment, I did not do this alone. I would like to thank my longtime friends Dave and Leslie Morris. Everyone should be blessed with friends who believe so deeply in them, and who know how to encourage the dreams of others. Without their support, I do not think this book would be a reality. Leslie, my editor and task master, kept me on target, and made my words flow gracefully onto the page when my ideas were stuck inside my head. Thank you.

Additionally, I would like to thank a few others who have directly inspired and/or contributed to this book: Carol Thompson, Alfred Macdaniel, Paul Grabowski, Tim Homan, Sam Decker, Steve Zager, Marny Lifshen, Harvey Mackay, Matt Lyons, Carmelo Gordian, Kelsey August, Custis Hoge, Cheryl Miller, John Egan, Amy Warmke, Brant Couch, Brian Fenske, Ed Kozun, and RW Rushing.

Bob Phelan, my father-in-law, deserves a huge thanks for his eagle eye in helping to proof the manuscript. There are many more people to whom I owe heartfelt thanks but there are simply not enough pages to thank everyone by name.

INTRODUCTION

Like many of you, my career has seen the highs and lows of a turbulent economy. In the six years prior to writing this book, I worked for three companies that either closed their doors completely or experienced heavy lay-offs. Tenacity, flexibility and creativity were musts in order for me to find new and challenging employment opportunities. I directly attribute a large part of my own success to utilizing the principles of networking that are discussed in this book.

Building a network of business contacts is one of the most important things you can do to help your career. Whether you want to grow in your current job or position yourself for a new opportunity, it's hard to make that leap on your own.

Some like to think that your personality is the only thing that will influence your ability to socialize in a business setting. They believe that only extraverts can effectively network. The reality is, however, that anyone can train him or herself to build professional relationships. The most important thing to remember is that while the purpose of networking is to gain more business opportunities for yourself, you must first do the reverse: help others.

I have made my share of mistakes in networking, and even failed to always follow the advice that I present in these pages. I do believe, however, that after more than a decade of being a proactive networker, others know that I am serious about this as an important part of anyone's business development plan. For these reasons I wrote this book.

Some Assembly Required: How to Make, Grow and Keep Your Business Relationships is based on the premise that people do business with people they know and like. While a lot of facts are weighed into a buying decision: price, quality, the company's longevity, etc., all other things being equal, customers will always choose the vendor that they have the best feeling about. In a world where more and more products and services are commoditized, having the advantage of being liked will become more and more important to career development.

The good news is that anyone can improve their ability to build strong relationships. The bad news is that no one can do it for you. That is why this book is called *Some Assembly Required*. Nothing in this book is as complex as rocket science or upper division algebra. The examples are things that anyone in any profession can do to stand apart from their competition. But you must take action.

The strategies presented on these pages may appear deceptively simple. Although they are basic, few professional businesspeople actually follow through and do these things. Workplace deliverables keep us so busy that it is easy to let relationships with clients, prospects, co-workers and others slip into a less important arena. But for those who can successfully cultivate these relationships, it makes the other burdens easier to carry. Individually, one person can only handle so much responsibility, but the more people who are by your side helping you succeed, the more you can accomplish.

Since the first edition of this book came out two years ago I have been fortunate to speak on networking at corporations, law firms, and business organizations around the United States. I have met executives at all levels who acknowledge that having a strong network is a key factor in their future success. Some have always practiced these principles, others are hungry for the know how to improve. In all cases they are inspired to cultivate true, mutually beneficial friendships with other people.

The feedback that I received from the first edition readers inspired me to add additional tips and stories to this new edition. While some things have changed, the overall message remains the same: to reach your highest potential you need others who honor, respect and assist you along your career path. Developing these types of relationships takes effort. Have you ever noticed that the center of the word "networking" is the word "work"? Yet when you master the skills in this book you will be amazed by the opportunities that will greet you.

Thom Singer
Austin, Texas, July 1, 2007

1

PEOPLE DO BUSINESS WITH

PEOPLE THEY KNOW AND LIKE

All things being equal, people do business with people they know and like. Prices can be matched but a decade-long friendship and a mutual admiration cannot. This is one reason top salespeople make big money; their longstanding client relationships bring in the deals. If the salesperson moves to a competitor, the business may very likely go with them. Chances are, if you have mastered the art of building strong relationships within your industry and community then you will never be out of a job.

A successful career requires a network

The most successful networker I know is mortgage broker Bob Stamatatos, whose company, Red Oak Capital, is in Burlingame, California. Bob has accomplished so much because, in addition to being a smart, nice guy, he understands the importance of building and cultivating a professional network.

He has worked with dozens of people I know on what is arguably the most important investment decision that they will ever make. And he does this in one of the most expensive and competitive housing markets in the country. Even in slow times, Bob's business continues to grow because his clients enthusiastically recommend him. He and his team treat people well, hold their hands through the stressful issues that always come with home financing, and share in their joy of a new home purchase. After the transaction closes, he stays in touch, often helping them find movers, painters, handy-men, etc. Bob is more than a mortgage broker, he is a trusted friend. People who have worked with him are quick to refer him because he has helped make their dream a reality. This is networking.

The many faces of networking

What exactly is networking? Networking is a word that many misunderstand and even more shy away from because they have a preconceived notion about it. They envision a pushy salesperson with slicked back hair trying to sell them a product that they have no interest in buying.

A network is having a lot of people who know and respect you, and understand your business. It is then easy for them to call on you if they need your product or service, or refer you to others because you are first in their mind when a need arises. By the same token, you understand their business and look for ways to send them work. A network is a give and take arrangement.

Building a network takes a big commitment and many people falsely think that they have no time in their schedule to do this. They claim that they are too busy to focus on anything other than the tasks at hand but, by doing so, they forget about the future. Many people have had life-changing career opportunities presented to them by people they knew well. Others have been introduced to large customers or other business leads directly from people they have come to know through their networking efforts.

If you attended a well-known business school you were probably introduced to networking early on; relationships with classmates and alumni are an important part of why people select certain universities for advanced degrees. There are many Harvard MBAs who keep in close contact with their classmates, and you can be sure that when a Harvard-educated CEO moves to a new company, members of his or her network will follow.

What networking is not

A good rule of thumb is that if you have known someone for less than three months, and have had less than five total interactions with them, they are not part of your network.

Networking is not connecting the dots between whom you know and whom they know. Using a friend's name without their consent can jeopardize both relationships. You may think that once you have established a close relationship with someone, his or her network is automatically your network. This is not true. Networking is not something you can do by yourself; it takes the participation and conscious help of others.

Networking is very different from cold calling. Real business relationships cannot be built just by phone, especially if they are one-sided. This does not mean that people you try to sell to cannot become part of your network, you just have to know the difference between selling and relationship building.

The Networking Quotient

Part of being able to improve your networking skills is to know where your strengths and weaknesses are in it. It's also nice to know how your efforts compare to others. Many people mistakenly believe that others share similar views and practices when it comes to networking. An avid networker thinks everyone takes relationships seriously, while the reluctant networker might assume everyone sees the practice as over-rated and bothersome.

To make any strides in this area, or any area of your life, you need to make a realistic assessment of where you are starting. Then you need to know in which areas and how to improve. Without this knowledge you will never know if you are making any progress.

For this reason I have created The Networking Quotient Quiz. This free, 30-question, online quiz will take you only eight minutes to complete. As you answer the questions, try hard to provide *your* answer, not the *right* answer.

The quiz allows you to assess how you react in a variety of networking situations. Moments after you answer the last question, you will receive your score and a comparison to others in your demographic areas.

Take the quiz at www.networkingquotient.com before you continue reading the rest of the book.

Just do it

Since it is hard to succeed in business without having some level of human contact, cultivating basic skills will help you stand out. If you sit back and wait for a network of influential people to materialize around you, plan for a long wait. Look around your own company. Are there people who have better relationships with co-workers, clients and the management team? Very often those with natural interpersonal skills excel while those who hide behind closed office doors do not. The fact that you have opened this book and read the first few pages is a sign that you believe in the power that other people can have on your career. As you progress through these chapters you will see that there is no magic bullet to propel you ahead. Your career will span many decades and at no point will you be done networking. Your network will always be evolving and changing. Building and maintaining connections with other people is a way of life, not just something to do on days that you have some extra time.

Marketing guru Seth Godin points out that the reason more people do not ride unicycles is because they do not come with training wheels. If they did, more people would learn to ride, and unicycle sales would boom.

Unfortunately, life has no training wheels. It would be nice if someone came along and showed you the way to balance career, marriage and parenting. But if you wait for that help, you will find yourself waiting for quite some time.

Instead, if you want something, just go and do it. Building your network simply requires that you take action. You'll take a few falls along the way but the bruise you gain from it is not the end of the world. Rather it teaches you just one more way not to do something. Get back up and try again.

Social networking

Linkedin.com, ryze.com and tribe.net are examples of online social networking services designed to help like-minded professionals link up. While these services can be great ways to find people and deliver information, technologies such as these will never replace traditional relationship building. They are just another tool that, if used properly, can expose you to people who share similar interests. Technology can help you manage your contacts, but in the end, relationship building has a strong personal component that cannot be circumvented.

See Chapter 5 for additional information on social networking.

Networking Myths

Myth 1: Networking is only for times when you are not busy.

Reality: There seems to be a boom and bust mentality around networking. People think that when business is good, they can ignore everyone around them, and that others will naturally understand that they are busy. Conversely, when things slow down, those people rally and try to pick up where they left off. In reality, if you fail to cultivate a relationship it will wither away. Jumping back into networking makes you seem flighty. No one is so busy that they cannot pick up the phone and call people on occasion. As long as you have to eat lunch, schedule it with someone that you want to keep in touch with. If you are too busy to pay any attention to other people you are either over-worked, ineffective or have an inflated view of your own self-importance.

Myth 2: Only senior executives need a network.

Reality: Everyone can benefit from having a professional network. For your current job, or for future employment opportunities, you must build your reputation now. No matter what your level or job function, affiliations with others only have an upside.

Myth 3: The people you meet networking never refer you business.

Reality: If you do for others, most of them will return the favor. I have had many experiences where people I have met through networking have directly given me business, referred business to me, recruited me to better jobs or become some of my closest friends. Case in point: my younger daughter's godmother is someone I met at a networking event.

Myth 4: Networking is unnecessary because if you are really good, the business will just come to you.

Reality: While this may be true, if you are the best-kept secret then you are leaving money on the table. Some people will hear of you because of your work alone, but if you are not actively helping advance your brand and your reputation, many other people will not even know you exist.

Myth 5: Decision makers never attend networking events.

Reality: Everyone goes somewhere. While the people you want to meet might not be at the same events that you attend, they are not all hermits. Additionally, other people in their firms or in their networks just might be there, and you may have a chance to get an introduction through someone else.

Networking and your Competition

Anyone who believes that they have no competition is either in a very unique business, or is fooling him or herself. Just because you do not have a competitor today does not mean that one will not emerge tomorrow. Advances in technology have made many industries more competitive. Consider the publishing and printing business. It was once true that the cost barriers to entry made it impossible for someone to self-publish a book and have a high-quality and cost-effective product. Yet the proliferation of desktop publishing and advances in printing technologies, not to mention the huge distribution changes via the Internet, have made such endeavors attainable to anyone.

Why strong relationships work to your advantage

In such a fast-paced and competitive environment, things that make you stand out from the crowd are not only important, they are crucial. The competition can always spend more money on advertising and marketing, and they can drop their price so low that it limits your ability to compete and still make a profit. If you have long-term relationships with your clients, and you provide ongoing value to them that goes beyond your product and service, the competition will have a long road ahead of them.

The devil you know

While it's not obvious, you should also network with the competition. Instead of viewing those whom you go up against as the enemy, consider the reasons you should know them:

It's good to have a "name with a face." You can be assured that in conversations with clients, prospects and others, their names will be tossed about. It is in your best interest to already know their strengths and weaknesses. Knowing your competition takes some of the fear out of competing with them. If they are the market leader, you already know that. If they give deep discounts, you know what's coming. If they are unethical, you are prepared for what they might be saying about you and your company. But at least you already know. A response of "Yes, I know them well" followed by some positive statement sets you above the fray. Regardless of what they say about you, it is in poor form to badmouth your competition. You won't win points by having negative words come out of your mouth, even if the person you are talking with is pushing the conversation in that direction.

Leads can come from the competitors. This is common in many industries. In law firms, for example, a firm could be ethically conflicted out of doing work for a client because of a pre-existing relationship with the adverse party. In such a case, a lawyer could be precluded from representing his top client in a matter. When this happens, it is in the firm's best interest to recommend another firm. In doing so, the attorney shows his commitment to the client, and can save the client a lot of time and effort in selecting the right lawyer. If the attorney has a good relationship with the firm he is introducing to his client, he can rest easier knowing that the other firm will not try to muscle in on the rest of the business.

Finding talent. As your own company grows and you need to find new employees, you can tap into your existing network. If you already know your competition, then you know who the superstars are within the industry. You know who has the right personality and work ethic to thrive inside your organization and it makes the hunt much easier, saving you time and recruiting fees.

Future employment. Similarly, it is not uncommon for other companies to look to their competition when opportunities arise within their organization. Much like we discussed above, having a tenuous relationship with your competitors could easily keep you off the short list for big career moves.

How you Conduct your Business

The core concept of networking to your business advantage is deceptively simple: all things being equal, people will always give their business with the person to whom they feel the best emotional connection. While they gather information on an analytical basis, in the end, they make decisions based on their gut feeling.

"All things being equal" is the nugget here. Naturally, people want quality and a good price. They want to be sure that the people they hire have the right credentials and experience, and that the products have a proven track record. But as long as these comparisons are the same, they will go with the person or the company that they know and trust.

Examine the products and services that you use. Like many other suburban Texans, my wife and I have a pest exterminator come to our house twice a year to spray for bugs. A quick check of our local phone book reveals dozens of pest control businesses. Why do we use this particular guy, a one-man shop without a brand name? It is simple. My neighbors have been his clients for ten years and when we noticed him there one day, I asked him to give us a quote. He seemed nice enough. We never have established a long-term contract with him, and yet, we have never shopped the business around to his competitors, some of which come from well-known national firms.

At the end of the day, his price seems right, bugs are never a problem, and when he comes to the house he is always very professional and he takes an interest in us. Is he our best friend? No. Do we know and like him? Yes. When we get coupons in the mail for his competition, we just toss them away. It is easier to go with the person that we have gotten to know and trust.

The Go To Person

Having a network makes you more valuable to others. People turn to you when they need information, not because they think that you know everything, but because they know that you will know where to find the answer.

Why would you want to be the Go To Person? Some might find it bothersome to frequently have people phone them with random inquiries. In reality, it depends on how you look at it. Is it an effort to answer the call or the email and then think about whom to direct the person to? Of course. But if one of your goals is to make yourself and your company first in the mind of others in the community, you've succeeded.

A while back, Texas Lawyer published a list of the Go To Lawyers in the state. A Go To Lawyer was named in the practice of civil litigation. Was he the best? It's hard to say. Yet he was chosen because, for the last 20 years, he had done a great job of building relationships with people inside and outside the legal community. From legal services to cigars to where to buy a car, he had connections and it never failed that when you mentioned his name, you received special attention. He did a great job of not only building a strong network but also going out of his way to connect those people.

The trick to being the Go To Person is not to be selfish. If you know someone who has a need, and you know another who provides a service, simply make the introduction without concern for what you get out of the deal. What goes around comes around. If you go out of your way to make connections, others will do the same for you. They may not be the same people you do for, but it all balances out in the end.

Internal Go To People have job security

In every company there is a person who knows how to handle all the little headaches that come up. From knowing how to operate the fax machine to knowing all the company holidays, this person pitches in and never gets caught up in the messy office politics or gossip. This is the Go To Person. The Go To Person has job security.

The person who knows how to get through all the red tape is far down on the list if layoffs should occur. Most managers have a certain person or two that they rely on to help make their job easier, and they protect those individuals as best they can during hard times.

Take Aways:

1. A successful career requires a network.

2. People do business with people they know and like.

3. Networking is a way of life, not something you do on days that you have extra time.

2

THE ACT OF NETWORKING:

NETWORKING IS NOT AN ACT

Successful people build networks by cultivating true, long-lasting relationships. Building solid business relationships on foundations of less than genuine intentions just doesn't work. People either know and trust you, or they don't. Because a relationship is solidified over a long period of time, those with less than sincere motives will eventually be sniffed out.

Make people a priority

When talking about networking, there are essentially three types of people:

Naturals. People with large networks share many characteristics. They like meeting new people and have an inherent curiosity about others. These natural networkers began doing this in childhood, long before they understood referrals, business plans or quotas. Instead, they just enjoy being around others.

Uncomfortable Networkers. Networking does not come as easily to these people but they have learned that they must network to grow their careers. They work to make other people a priority. It's a little harder for them to make interpersonal connections but they succeed by putting in a little more work than does a natural networker.

Selfish or ignorant people. These people are annoyed by those who cannot help them and generally ignore them altogether because they are caught up in their own needs. Many selfish people do become very successful, and they never acknowledge that others have contributed to their success. We all know people like this: their sole interaction is with those from which they see immediate payoff.

You've been networking for far longer than you realize

Here's one more way to look at it. It's your child's first day of kindergarten. Do you tell him or her to go to school, not talk to anyone and play alone at recess? No. You give him or her a little pep talk on going, having a good time, making some new friends, and being polite to the teacher. This is networking in its most basic form.

From the early days on the playground you began making connections and forging friendships. Some of these relationships were stronger than others. Some were tumultuous. Others were joyous and beneficial. Most were somewhere in between. The point: you have been meeting people since you spoke your first words.

A few years ago I went to the wedding of a kindergarten classmate. It was absolutely amazing how many childhood friends the groom, now in his early 40s, had in attendance. While the groom and I are not as close today as we were in Miss O'Brien's class, I cannot recall a time when he was not my friend. The groom is a good example of a natural networker.

Anyone can refer business

You never know who can and will refer business so to out-of-hand dismiss a certain type of person leaves you coming up short. Not everyone you meet will become part of your network and not everyone will become your friend. Not everyone will understand your business or place any effort into helping others. That's okay because your mission is to connect with those who are like-minded. Keep in mind that someone else's success in no way diminishes your own—even those with whom you compete. To let someone else's victory bring you down is to waste time that you could better use for fine-tuning your own strategy.

Bryan is the CEO of his fourth technology start-up. He is often approached to join the Young Presidents' Organization or networking groups for senior executives. Instead, he started a group made up of individuals of all levels in marketing, sales, law and insurance. He also included some entrepreneurs. His theory was that his company's needs might not always be solved by someone who was his peer but that a cross-section of people in business would bring many good connections and points of view that he might not otherwise be exposed to. This group met monthly for two years and at each meeting every attendee had to talk about what his or her largest challenge was that month. Help often came from the least expected person. If, for example, a company needed a new receptionist, another CEO would never sing the praises of his own receptionist, but a sales person or HR executive just might do so to help their friend, the receptionist, find a better opportunity. Bryan believed that having your network go from top to bottom was more helpful than just knowing those on top.

Reasons why people don't network

Meeting people and building a business network is not something that happens by itself; it takes focus, effort and a time commitment. Here are two common reasons people avoid networking.

1. **I'm too busy.** While it is true that there is little free time in business, time spent building a network of contacts is an investment in the future.

2. **Am I worthy?** Self-doubt is another excuse for avoiding connecting with others. This is silly, of course, because the point of networking is showing others what you can bring to the table. People want to know who you are. Anyone with a contact database can find plenty of examples of people who came on the scene with a lot of pizzazz yet never amounted to anything. If you prove that you are reliable, will be around for a while, and intend to help others, people will want to know you.

No one will do it for you

Networking is not something that you can delegate to your secretary or to the new guy down the hall. As much as you may see it as a difficult task that you would rather ignore, if you're in a business where benefit comes from knowing other people then you are the only one who can build your own network. Invest the time to meet people and then invest more time to get to know them. Conversely, you can let your competitor do it.

Tracy, a lawyer, once told me that, while she wanted to expand her practice, she did not want to invest any additional time or energy into networking. She wanted me, the firm's marketing manager, to do something to make her phone ring. Her belief was that our firm was not running enough advertisements on her specialty, and that was why she did not have enough business. I explained to her that advertising was a tool to give the firm some recognition and that knowing the name of the firm would help them to connect with her. But to win in a relationship sales environment, she needed to build relationships, and there were no shortcuts. She needed to build that trust.

To come out on top in a business where relationships win the business, you need to start early and keep at it. Those at the top of the relationship game do not stop, they simply work harder at it. Hard work? Yes! But it is a much better ride than going it alone.

Networking for when you lose your job

Some months ago I got a call from a friend of a friend. She had been laid off from a large computer manufacturer in Austin and she was not having any luck finding new employment. Two months had passed and, with a slow job market, she saw no prospects for employment. Many of her co-workers had already landed in new positions, and she discovered that all of them had found their opportunities through someone they knew.

She had not ever given any credit to networking. In fact, she had always discredited it as "fluff" and thought it only for people with free time. She was a workaholic, convinced that if she worked hard and met her quota, she would never be laid off.

She was wrong.

Now that she needed a job, she was behind candidates who had an "in" for the few coveted openings. And so we had coffee. Here is what happened:

1. She invited me, then made it clear that she expected me to pick up the check since I was employed.

   If you invite someone to coffee or lunch you should expect to pick up the bill. If the person offers to pay, you can decide if it is appropriate but do not assume that because you are out of work, your guest should buy your lunch.

2. She was not grateful for my time. I had never met this woman before and yet I spent an hour listening to her situation. Networking is not free therapy. She mistakenly assumed that since I was a Natural Networker, that our time together was no big deal. She never said "thank you" when we parted and I never received any follow up from her. Not surprisingly, I have never seen her again.

If you are going to be serious about networking to help you find your next job you need to start before you become unemployed! However, if you are starting late, you need to realize that building a network takes time. If you do meet someone with a large network, be respectful that it is their network (not yours), and do not expect them to just introduce you (a stranger) to important people that they know.

Finally, be thankful (very thankful!) to anyone who talks with you about your quest. People are more likely to help someone who is genuinely grateful than someone who just expects help from the rest of the planet.

You are always "on"

Celebrities and professional athletes are often photographed doing things that do not help promote their image. They defend their less-than-admirable actions by complaining that they were not "on." While a person who is well-networked in the business community is not stalked by the paparazzi, they are still subject to the same scrutiny as anyone with a recognizable face. If you are committed to building a responsible reputation, don't mess it up by doing something damaging, even when on your own time.

I once attended a college football game with an attorney from a well-regarded law firm. After the game we went to a local bar where this young lawyer had a few too many beers and proceeded to make a fool of himself. His biggest blunder was when I introduced him to a partner at another law firm, who was standing with one of his clients, a local CEO. After polite introductions, the associate handed his card to the CEO and proclaimed, "When you are ready to work with a real law firm, give me a call." His drunken humor fell on deaf ears. The CEO looked shocked and the other lawyer was appalled. While both of them laughed about it, it was clear that this person had hurt his own reputation, and that of the firm he worked for. Chances are, if that associate ever needs a job, he will not end up at the firm where this partner works.

People have lost clients because they openly conducted extramarital affairs or displayed other outward lapses of character. When they find out the reason they have lost the business, they are shocked that anyone was watching what they did in their personal lives and letting that cloud their business decisions. If you show someone that you are dishonest in one way, they assume you will be dishonest in others. If you think there are separate worlds between one's personal conduct and their business conduct, you are mistaken. Character counts.

With that in mind, remember that you are responsible for your reputation and the reputation of the company you work for. This means always and not just from nine to five on weekdays. While this may seem unfair or too much of a burden to carry, it is fact.

"Integrity is the basis of trust." [1]

—*Warren Bennis*

The Fun Factor

All this talk about the amount of time and effort that go into building a strong network can take the focus off the fact that this should be fun. For naturally gregarious people, making friends and building long-lasting, mutually beneficial relationships is just part of daily life. For people who are more introverted, the level of attention it takes to do such things can be tedious. And for those that would rather stay in their office and research or write reports, networking can be downright painful. But if you are convinced that having a network can and will benefit your career, you might as well have a good time in the process, regardless of the amount of effort it requires. Realize that other people are part of your path to success and go out and discover them.

---

1 Warren Bennis, *On Becoming a Leader* (Perseus Publishing, 1992) page 164

Most people have an interesting story to tell. Think of
this as unraveling an amazing puzzle. People like to and
will talk about themselves, their experiences and their
aspirations if they think the other person is truly interested.
Learn where they grew up, where they went to college.
Have they traveled extensively? How did their career path
lead them to where they are today? Are they married?
Do they have children? It's easy to become so focused on
someone's professional attributes that we forget that they
are more than just the CFO of a manufacturing company.

Treat your interactions with others as an exploration. Each
day try to learn one thing new about someone. Consider it
your own secret game; you win if, on your commute home,
you can think of one personal quality you learned about
someone you spoke with.

Many of the business events you will attend are social in
nature. When people inquire how you're doing, have ready
a positive response. If asked how business is going, give a
response like "It's great, and I look forward to it getting
better." Steer clear of answers such as "Well, it's okay,
but we do not nearly have the amount of new business
that we want to have." The latter sends a strong message
that things are not going well where you work. Subtle
comments and the optimism in your voice speak louder
than anything else you can say.

*"Questions persuade more powerfully than any
other form of verbal behavior, so you should
develop a set of questions that you are comfortable
with and that allow you to work in your personal
comfort zone in showing your sincere interest
in others."* [2]

—Zig Ziglar

Finding the right mix

Building a network is not about going out into the
community and meeting people who will immediately
hand you new business or career opportunities. If it were
that easy then everyone would be doing it. Rather than
be of the mindset that everyone you meet should and will
impact your career, view it as an ongoing process where
you meet people, get to know them and assist them when
you can, never knowing who will come through for you
in the long run.

Consider the Pork Chop Man. Every time the Pork Chop
Man meets someone who could possibly be a client or refer
him business, he acts as if he were a hungry wolf and they
have a pork chop hanging around their neck. Networking

2 Zig Ziglar, *Ziglar on Selling* (Ballantine Books, 1993), page 156

is never about devouring the other person for your own gain, rather it is about having connections to many different people whom you like and respect, and who feel the same about you. It's about mutually finding ways to assist each other when the opportunity arises.

Let's say that you have the opportunity to meet five new people at each event you attend. Attending one event a week would mean you could meet 20 people a month or 140 a year. But not all of those people will be ones that you want to get to know better, or who want to get to know you. In reality, over time you might have the ability to turn only one or two of those you meet each month into strong enough relationships that you could consider them part of your network.

It takes years to successfully build a strong network

One of the most important personal traits you need to successfully create a working network is patience. More often than not, people want you to prove yourself before you join their inner circle. Just as you would not invite a near stranger to Thanksgiving Dinner, people do not welcome you into their network after an initial meeting. Quota pressures can make you want to push relationships along faster in order to achieve more sales in the short term. But to really build relationships takes time. This means months to some and years to others. Let the friendship develop at its own pace. Forcing the relationship will rarely lead to the long-term commitment you seek.

Does that mean that if you are pushy you won't be successful in business? No. Not all business requires a strong relationship in order to close a sale. However, if you know that your business is relationship-based, then taking a short-term view will not be in your best interest. There are plenty of those ignorant, selfish people we discussed at the beginning of this chapter who care nothing for others and who have successful, financially rewarding careers. Bottom line: do you really want to be one of them?

Take Aways:

1. *It takes years and a sustained commitment to create a network.*

2. *No one can do it for you.*

3. *Character counts.*

3

THE BLUEPRINT:

ARCHITECTING YOUR PLAN

Many people get out of bed every day and just let their careers happen. They talk about wanting a better job, or more money, but they just sit back and wait. These well-educated, seemingly ambitious people have given little thought to what they need to do to get more from their working life and, instead, proceed through their careers without a plan.

The Strategy

Would you build a house without a set of blueprints? Let's imagine what that house would look like. No matter how good of a carpenter you were, and even if you had all the right building materials, you would end up with a disaster.

A plan is simply a vision for the end result. It allows you to make sure you have all the pieces in place to accomplish the project. When building a home you would know that you need to think about plumbing before you pour the foundation. You would know in advance if that house would have one story or two. With no plan, your house would be condemned before you could ever move in.

Getting started

You have heard of the Six Degrees of Separation Theory? The Kevin Bacon parlor game? While this might be fun over a glass of wine at a dinner party, in the business world, if you are more than two degrees away, you can be relatively sure that you are not close enough to reap the benefits. Thus, it is important to know whom you need to know, and get to know them.

First, you need to know what type of contacts you want to have and where to meet these types of people. If your clients are bankers then you will have a different plan than if your clients are doctors. One of the most common mistakes that people make in attempting to build a network is that they think it's solely a numbers game. While anyone can refer you business, you still need to be strategic in whom you meet.

Who are your clients?

The question "Who are your clients?" is often answered with a protective, suspicious response of "Why do you need to know?" People seem to think that sharing a client list opens them up to theft of those clients. While broadcasting your client list to your competition is not in your best interest, a smart competitor already knows who is not their client, and is plotting to gain that business.

Why ask then? The best way to determine whom you should be targeting for new business comes from knowing who is currently buying your services. If you know why someone is your client, and what makes them stay your client, it is easier to replicate those same successes.

If you already know who your clients are, fantastic! If you don't, then set aside some time to figure this out. How can you attract more clients who will be just as great to work with and just as profitable?

Exercise 1 – Top Clients

Make a list of your 10 top clients. Top can be determined any way you choose; one way to do this is to take your ten largest clients in terms of revenue. After listing them, jot down a few bullets about how they first became your clients, and why you think they continue to stay with you. Finally, is there any other product your firm offers that they are currently not buying or worse, buying from a competitor?

Company	Business Development Method	Cross-Selling Opportunities
1.		
2.		
3.		
4.		
5.		
6.		
7.		
8.		
9.		
10.		

Now, review the list for patterns. Digest this and determine how you can use this information to gain business from similar companies.

Finally, review the areas where you can sell additional services to your existing customer. If this will involve others in your firm, do not hesitate to call upon your co-workers and strategize how to quickly get in front of the client.

Lisa, who sold surgical tools, worked with eight of 15 hospitals in a major metropolitan area. They had been her customers for over a decade and her business had remained impressive but flat. Over time, many of the more junior people she had known had moved to higher-level positions with the other hospitals, yet she had not actively maintained relationships with those people. The opportunity for growth was made clear to her by looking at who her largest clients were, and then looking to others in the industry she already knew. She already had some level of a relationship with buyers in almost all 15 hospitals, but, because she had failed to cultivate these relationships when the people had changed employers, these were not strong connections. After discovering this, Lisa created a plan to expand her business by reaching out to everyone who had formerly worked for her clients. In doing so, she was able to open doors into hospitals that had traditionally been loyal to her competitors.

Whom do you want as a client?

Knowing what kind of companies you want as clients will make it easier for you to recognize them when they are in front of you. If you are focused on this even when you are busy, you will be on the lookout for new companies that you can work with. It's a challenge. When you're franticly working on a high-priority task, it's common to ignore even the simplest things to build relationships and attract clients. It's easy to fall into the trap of thinking that what is currently on your plate is more important than everything else in your life. Be cognizant of letting today's pressures fully outweigh your continuing commitment to building your business. You do not want to be stuck when the economy slows down and end up on a panicked mission to revive your network. Even when you are busy, you can carve out the time in your schedule to cultivate your relationships.

Martin, a travel agent, is very focused on his customer service. He forgets to eat or sleep while making complicated travel plans for his sophisticated, demanding corporate clients. While this dedication to his customers is admirable, it is not a realistic way to build a profitable business. When he gets busy, he forgets to check his email, does not return phone calls and fails to do the simple tasks that help lead to new business. The solution? He now schedules a minimum of 30 minutes every day to send emails to prospects and set up networking lunches. Carving out 30 minutes a day for these tasks has helped Martin eliminate the slow periods in his business.

Exercise 2 – Wish List

Take out a piece of paper and list every company that you would like to work with. Use tools like your local "Book of Lists" or national industry directories to assist you in coming up with names. Don't stop until you have at least 50. This is your Wish List.

Company
1.
2.
3.
4.
5. and so on

Exercise 3 – Target List

Now, determine which companies you should focus your efforts on. Your goal is to turn your large Wish List into a 20-company Target List. You can have more companies than that in your pipeline, but it's likely you can only do a good job of going after a maximum of 20 at a time.

Company	Existing Contact?	Priority (A / B / C)
1.		
2.		
3.		
4.		
5. and so on		

Look at your Wish List and flag all the companies where you already have a contact. This could be someone who used to work at a current client or someone you know socially. "Know" is defined as someone that you could pick up the phone and call to say hello, and they would know right away to whom they were speaking.

Your next step is to identify those companies where you think you could easily make connections. It's okay now to highlight a company where the CFO went to your same college, albeit ten years earlier. He or she is not necessarily a friend or acquaintance, but if you had a chance meeting, you would have something to talk about.

Finally, identify those companies where you just have a good gut feeling. From those companies, select between 10 and 20 to make part of your Target List.

Now, write them down and prioritize them using A, B or C, based on what level of relationship already exists. For those that you already have an existing relationship with, pick up the phone and make contact today. Right now. Ask if you can come and talk with them about your business and how you can work together.

Share your list

Share your Target List with the people you work with. Often, multiple people in the same company are pursuing a prospect without shared knowledge of it. Equally as bad is one person pursuing a prospect, when another person within their organization has a strong relationship with them and would be happy to help facilitate an introduction.

It is always better to have multiple points of contact with a prospective company. You are just one person and cannot possibly build relationships and maintain contact with every decision maker at every company. In addition, no matter how good you are at making connections, you will not build strong bonds with everyone you meet. Because of this, the more people you have on your side working on the same prospects, the more successes you will ultimately have.

Looking for opportunities

Here's where your network comes into play. You need to be looking for opportunities to meet people at the companies on your Target List. The hard part is figuring out which of your contacts know the right influential individuals. How do you secure an introduction? While you may have strong enough relationships with some people to just call and ask, with others you will need to look for creative ways to get them to help you.

Having regular conversations with your business contacts about whom they want as clients, as well as sharing your Target List, will create a situation where others are also looking for ways to help you. A successful sales professional, by definition, lets people in his network know whom he has strong relationships with, and whom he wants to get to know. He asks his contacts if they know any of his targets, and offers to make introductions for them. Even if his contacts do not know anyone, they will think of him months later when they happen across someone who can be of assistance. He is always looking for new opportunities for himself and for those in his network, and others look out for him as well. This is how an optimal network operates. Everyone helps each other.

Follow up and knowing what success looks like

When individuals and organizations have the urge to accomplish more and grow their business, they give a lot of lip service to discovering their strengths and overcoming weaknesses, making grand plans to have a business development focus. They then wake up from their dream and face a large number of new emails, an in-box full of important papers, phone calls to make, and office politics to overcome. Their Target List gets filed (round or otherwise) and they don't think about their plan until the next time that they get hit with that feeling that they can do more.

You see it in every work situation. The process of making a plan and identifying prospects supersedes the actual action involved with turning that plan into reality. Firms spend significant dollars hiring highly paid trainers and consultants, they send countless executives to training programs, they read dozens of books on business topics, and yet they do not emphasize follow up.

Fact: A goal that is not acted on is a wish.

The final part of your plan is recognizing when you have achieved success. With respect to attaining new clients, success can be defined by the number of new clients or the dollar amount of sales. If part of your long-term strategy is to grow your visibility, then success is harder to quantify. You might count your wins by the amount of media coverage you receive. Knowing more people can be good, but for most, just having a network is not worth much unless it converts to revenue opportunities. If your true goal is new clients and increased sales, then making new friends inside your target companies is not a success until they buy your product or service.

Setting Career Goals

Where are you on your career path today? Where would you like to be in five years? If you do not have a definitive answer, you are not alone. Many people do not know this. Yet as the business landscape gets more competitive, you cannot just wait for success to come to you.

Think of it this way. If you were going to plant a garden, you would not just throw a bunch of unidentified seeds around a patch of dirt. You would have to know how you want the garden to look and what type of plants would be appropriate for the climate where you live. Just tossing seeds around would give you no guarantee that the plants would grow at all, and if they did grow, you would not know what kind of plants you were going to get. You might get a whole garden of weeds. However, this is the approach that many people take with their livelihood.

Begin with the end in mind

Think about how you want your career to progress. Start by assessing where you are and how you got here. You made choices that have led to your current situation. This could be where you chose to go to college, the industry you work in, or how far up the proverbial corporate ladder you have already climbed.

For example, if you are a sales representative and you want to become a sales manager, you can start to make choices that will lead you toward that goal. That being said, it does not need to be overly specific because situations change and new opportunities arise, so you need to build in some flexibility to your goals.

Create a series of short- and long-term goals

These goals should be realistic and clearly defined. Write them down on a piece of paper and put them somewhere where you can refer to them regularly. Quantify them. You may want to tape them to your bathroom mirror, or put them on the visor in your car.

Some examples of goals include: reading one book each month, taking two industry-related courses each year, and completing the continuing education necessary to maintain your professional certifications.

Thom's System:
At the beginning of each year I write down my goals. Then
I laminate them and keep them in my wallet where I'll
frequently see them.

Take action

Once you have identified what you want, do it! The hardest part is taking the first step. After that, it's momentum.

I spent years thinking about writing this book. While I had written dozens of articles for business and marketing publications, writing a book seemed like too daunting of a task. Then I made it a goal. I wrote it down. I talked to people about it. I found someone to coach me through the project. We mapped out a plan and then I took that first step to commit words to paper. In the beginning it was hard to find the time to write and I was not happy with the way the words came out. But each day I looked at my goal, and I took action. Within a few weeks it became more fun to do, and I was happier with the quality of the work. Then I started to look forward to working on it and then a chapter was completed. I had created a road map toward a book. I set a defined list of targeted goals and I followed up with action. I knew what the end result would look like, and you are holding that realized goal in your hand right now.

Share with others what your future achievement will look like. You are not out there in the world all alone. You have friends, family and a professional network of contacts. You have a mentor or a peer group who has agreed to help you find your way. You never know when telling people what you want to accomplish can lead to their showing you a new way to pursue your dreams.

Take Aways:

1. *Study how you originally got your current clients, and look for ways to replicate this.*

2. *Share your Target List with co-workers and others in your network*

3. *Set goals then take action.*

4

THE NUTS AND BOLTS:
BUILDING RELATIONSHIPS

People tend to view their personal relationships and business relationships very differently. They feel a kinship toward their social friends, but do not always have the same affinity toward those they know professionally. It is, however, just as important to put in the effort to building business relationships as it is with your social circle. A person you know through work has the same feelings and human needs as anyone else. If you really care about the people you meet, regardless of the situation, it will show. When you make other people feel important and let them know you care, they will be drawn to you. To successfully build any relationship requires effort and the occasional sacrifice.

The Dating Game

Are you dating your customers or are you married to them?

This is a confusing question. The United States divorce rate borders on 50%. Therefore being married is not as much of a long-term commitment as some might think. Think about marriage. Dating someone involves looking around for things to do for them: nice meals, fun outings, gifts, etc. Married people begin to take their spouses for granted. The courtship phase is over! Before marriage one wonders if their spouse will stay around for the long term, and so that intensifies their interest in keeping their mate happy and progressing the relationship to the next level.

Treat your clients this way. Be excited to find ways to serve them and make them happy. Ask questions about how the relationship is going, much the way you might ask someone you've been dating six months.

Using the dating analogy, here are some things to remember when building relationships with your clients.

The first date

This may take place at the suggestion of a third party, similar to a blind date. Someone you each know thinks that you could be mutually helpful to each other in a business context, and suggests that you meet. The introduction could come in person, by phone or by email. Another possibility is that you just meet by happenstance but, while talking, realize that the conversation should be continued at another time.

Whenever you meet them, listen more than you talk. People who enjoy the personal side of networking usually are outgoing and like to talk. It's common for one person to dominate the conversation and spend the whole time waxing poetic about themselves and their business. To prevent this, make listening and asking questions the top priority of your first encounter. Find out where they work, what their role is in that organization, how long they have worked there, and where they were previously, or what path led them to that job. In addition, try to learn what types of individuals or businesses make up their client list.

In most cases, the other person will follow up by asking you similar questions. This is what you want. Plan ahead about how you describe your business and what role you play. The short, memorized description is often referred to as an elevator pitch. (If you were on the 25th floor of a building and someone asked you what you did for a living, could you clearly and concisely describe it before you reached the lobby?)

A strong answer would be:

"I am the business development manager for PhoenixSoft, one of the city's fastest growing, privately held software companies. We have four offices in the US and one in London, and we work with companies ranging from emerging growth and venture-backed enterprises to publicly traded Fortune 100 companies."

Having thought it out in advance and knowing the core message allows you to change up the exact wording depending on the person you are talking with. It also frees you up to be thinking of the next question you have for the other person. If you can keep them talking, you will discover ways that you can be beneficial to them. The more people talk about themselves, the more they often enjoy the conversation, which will lead to additional encounters.

The second date

When dating for romance, there are many first dates but far fewer second dates. The same is true in the business world. Sometimes you will have an instant connection with people and immediately find ways to collaborate. Sometimes there will be people that you meet and slowly build such a connection with over a long period of time. There will be those people whom you simply do not like and can think of no reason to ever talk to them again. Finally, there will be those people who clearly do not like you.

Yes, it is true. They may not like you. There was an episode of Seinfeld where someone simply didn't like Jerry. Jerry's mother was incredulous and kept asking, "How can someone not like Jerry??!" It happened to Jerry and in time, it will happen to you. It is best that you accept it up front, because, if you have a large enough network, it is inevitable. In these cases, be polite when you see those people and move on. Do not waste time trying to change their mind. Even more importantly, refrain from gossiping about that person to others. If someone asks you about them, just change the subject.

Focus on the positive. If you are sincere in the manner with which you treat people and if you find ways to assist others in meeting their goals, then you will have more positive interactions than you can ever imagine.

Moving the relationship forward

For most, the goal of dating is to move the relationship toward marriage. A business relationship is different because the courtship phase never ends. You need to find ways to add value and find reasons to continue to interact. This is another reason why knowing what is important to the other person, both professionally and personally, is so important. The more you know about your clients, the more you can find ways to be a solution to their problems. By looking for ways to positively help those around you, by default you will advance the relationship.

Your goal in any business relationship is to give more than you take. If you think that someone else's success somehow limits your own potential then you are dead wrong. Personal and career success, and happiness and wealth, are all unlimited.

The Golden Rule

You're no doubt familiar with the Golden Rule: Do unto others as you would want them to do unto you.

Let's start inside the company you work for. Think about the people you encounter on a daily basis. Surely there's someone who is arrogant, selfish, demanding and rude. It's not you but, rather, someone that you interact with on a regular basis. Do you look forward to helping that person? Would you go out of your way to let them know information that could be beneficial to them?

More often than not, what goes around comes around. If you are not treating people with respect then that, in turn, will damage your reputation. Titles alone do not command respect; respect is earned. Additionally, you cannot pick and choose, treating your superiors and peers one way, while demeaning your subordinates. People notice and they will not trust you.

Too many people, too little time

A well-connected, friendly person will always have a lot of people trying to get on his or her calendar. One of my childhood friends worked hard to climb the corporate ladder at his prestigious employer. Our friendship had spanned several decades and there was no reason for me to think we wouldn't stay close. Post-college, my friend and I were on very different paths. Still, I continued to reach out to him. When I did finally reach him by phone he told me that his busy schedule only allowed time for people who could help him in business and since I was "just a photographer," he hoped I understood that he would not have time for me. Ouch.

The silver lining was the valuable lesson I took away: treat everyone with respect. I would not want another person to go through what I did when my childhood friendship ended.

While you do not need to make time for everyone, you can be creative in ways you handle demands on your time. Ignoring someone or telling them flat out that they do not make the cut is just not nice.

In the 1990s I sold advertising for the Austin Chamber of Commerce. One gentleman whom I wanted to meet with had balked that he was too busy but, when I persisted, he invited me to his office for 30 minutes at 6 a.m. Of course I

went. He confided to me that he offers the 6 a.m.
time slot to people all the time and that most of them
turn him down. The lesson here: it is a great way to weed
through who is serious about having a meeting and who
is not. I often offer to meet with people for coffee at
7 a.m. It is amazing how many people find excuses not to
do this and that's fine. It allows me to make the offer of
my time politely without adversely impacting my schedule.
Fortunately I am a morning person and my local Starbucks
opens at 6 a.m.

Give First

There is a common thread that runs through every topic in
this book: building a successful business network requires
putting others first. While history reveals many examples
of legendary tyrants, there are better ways to do business.

Most people who have reached great success in their career
genuinely enjoy the people they do business with. They
make it a habit of giving of themselves before they ask
others to assist them.

"If there is any single rule to follow in networking circumstances, it is not 'How can I get the other person to do something for me?' It's 'How can I do something for the other person?'" [3]

—*Harvey Mackay*

Here's one strategy: Instead of being the new guy in the organization who chimes in with an opinion at every meeting, spend the first year listening. Volunteer behind the scenes. Take the jobs no one else wants like setting up or working the registration table at an event. If you remain quiet and help other people for a whole year, when you do step up and voice your thoughts, everyone will listen.

In the early stages of relationships it's easy to talk too much and to alienate others. Leaders in a company or a volunteer organization get very little support for the "heavy lifting," thus they tend to be grateful to those who are willing to do the less glamorous jobs, especially if they are not clamoring for the public kudos.

"There is no limit to what a man can do or where he can go if he doesn't mind who gets the credit."

—*Raymond Eisenhardt Sr.*

---

3 Harvey B. Mackay, *Dig Your Well Before You're Thirsty* (Currency, 1999) page 154

Open your network to others

Once a quarter, look at your contact database and give some thought to those who would benefit from knowing each other. Here are two easy ways to do this:

1. Pick out five people whom you feel strongly about and search for those it would be mutually beneficial for them to get to know.

2. Pick the five newest additions to your network and specifically search through your database to see whom you can introduce them to.

Either way, make a habit of linking up people. Everyone wins when you do this.

Networking as a bank account

Stephen R. Covey's concept of the emotional bank account, which he writes about in his *New York Times* bestseller *The 7 Habits of Highly Effective People*, is equally true in networking. You have to make deposits with people. For example, you can invite them to your company's events. You can introduce them to important people in the community. Simply saying nice things about people around town goes a long way. Have you ever thought poorly of anyone who said nice things about others?!

Only after you have built up this goodwill with others will you have the ability to ask them for favors. But, like a bank account, you need to plan your withdrawals carefully to avoid becoming overdrawn. Similar to how a bank regards customers who bounce checks, people frown at those who take more than they give. It's a careful balance. Make it a priority to not become overdrawn with the people you have in your network. If you do find yourself in a situation where you have received a lot of help from an individual, and have not had the opportunity to be of assistance to them, tell them that you recognize the situation and ask if there is anything you can do for them. Thank them. Even if there is nothing you can do to equalize the situation, by simply thanking the other person and acknowledging it, you will have made some headway on clearing the outstanding balance. A sincere thank you is worth a lot.

Keep track of your balance. You would not leave your money in a bank that paid you no interest and treated you poorly, while charging fees along the way. The same is true with people. Eventually someone will take advantage of you or simply not help you when it is within their power to do so. Accept that this is just part of doing business.

The Follow-Up

While many business people regularly attend networking functions, few of them actually succeed in adding people to their network. Simply meeting a person does not give you the right to claim that relationship as part of your network. I once met a woman who ran a public relations agency. We had a brief, pleasant conversation. The next day she called my employer and introduced herself as a friend of mine, suggesting that they meet to discuss my firm's public relations needs. From my perspective this was inappropriate because, not only were we not friends, she had not asked my permission to use my name as part of her introduction. If she had invested the time in building a relationship with me, I might have spoken to my employer on her behalf.

You cannot skip steps in relationship building. There is no quick way, nor is there a formula for exactly how long it will take. Building your network is no different than making social friends. Working on the relationship takes time; it takes effort on both sides, but, since many people are not as focused on this as you are, more of the effort may be on your shoulders. There's a fine line between reaching out to people and being pushy. Friendships develop at their own pace. If you feel that you are not making progress with someone, or that they do not like you, move on.

During the technology boom of the late 1990s you could fill an entire day with networking functions. "Three Nametag Days" meant you would be at a different event for breakfast, lunch and dinner. But for many, these were simply places to eat and drink, and have a legitimate excuse to fill out an expense report. They attended because they were told that networking was an important thing for their career, but they never asked why or how.

Without follow-up, business rarely comes from networking. The easy part is meeting people. Many mistake the "meeting" for the whole networking process, and wrongly confuse a new acquaintance with a business friend. The truth is that the follow-up and the building of a legitimate relationship is the most critical.

The morning after

Let's assume that you are committed to participating in the community and that you are great at meeting people and learning enough about them to determine if it's worthwhile to take the next step. You leave events proud of how many exciting and dynamic people you have met.

What's next? Put those business cards in a safe place! It's common for networking events to take place after business hours. After you go home, make sure that you remove all of the cards you collected from your pocket or purse. Take a moment to review the cards and make specific notes about the person or your conversation. You may even want to note at which event you met. If you do not immediately develop a friendship with the other person, it is not uncommon that your paths will cross again, sometimes years later. If you can immediately recall where you met the first time, it's a positive signal to the other person that you noticed them. In addition, if you save cards, or later transfer the information to a database and review that info periodically, it will help trigger your memory.

The next day, when you prepare to leave for work, be sure to take the cards with you. It's easy to leave the cards from a previous evening's event on the kitchen counter and have one of your young children relocate them. It's just as easy for an unsuspecting spouse or housekeeper to erroneously throw them away. Your goal is to get the cards to the office where the information can be quickly transferred into a database and/or the card can be saved in its designated place.

Thom's System:
I enter all the information into my computer and also save the physical card in a business card file notebook. These files are inexpensive binders that can be purchased at any office supply store. I often skim through the pages to refresh my memory about people that I might have lost touch with or need to reconnect with. While this can be done by scanning the database, there is something about seeing their physical business cards and company logos that helps jog my memory.

A follow-up note

After you have met people, it's important that you find a way to connect with them again. Although there are many ways to do this, one of the simplest and most unassuming ways is to send them a short note. This can be done by either email or by a handwritten note. A quick, handwritten note has a powerful impact. The only arguments in favor of using email are immediacy and ease of use. It is also, in today's business world, the more common way to send a follow-up note, however, it is not as memorable as a handwritten note.

Here's an example:

Dear Dennis,

It was a pleasure to talk with you at the Chamber of Commerce dinner. I enjoyed learning about your company and wish you much continued success. Please let me know if I can ever be of any assistance.

Brian

The purpose of such a note is simply to let the other person know that you enjoyed meeting them. Enclose your business card even if you gave it to them when you met since there's a good chance that your card never made it back to their office. By enclosing another card you are making it easier for them to remember you.

"Word-processed notes are too easy to create from a template and easy to delegate to a secretary. Handwritten notes clearly show that the person was worth your time." [4]

—Harry Beckwith

4 Harry Beckwith, *What Clients Love* (Warner Business Books, 2003) page 230

Since I began my career, I have made it a habit to write between five and ten notes each week. Because so few people take the time to write notes, people often comment on my handwritten notes. It makes it easy for them to start a conversation the next time I see them, or gives them an excuse to send me an email. This starts a dialogue and that leads toward building a relationship.

A few years ago I decided to track how many others did this same thing. I put a shoebox under my desk and placed every note I received in the box after I had read it. By December, not including holiday cards, I had 33 notes in the box, which was less than 10% of the number that I sent out. This solidified my belief that, by taking the time to acknowledge people with a note, I would stand out from the crowd.

Future follow-up

Beyond making initial contact by sending a short note, if the person is clearly someone that you want to get to know further then you need to plan for future follow-up. The trick here is to not be too pushy. If you force it by sending a note and then immediately calling to schedule coffee or lunch, the other person may not feel comfortable, especially if they did not feel the same about you.

If you are active in the business community, chances are that you will cross paths with people fairly regularly. This gives you the opportunity to talk a few times, and then suggest that you get together for coffee. If the person agrees, scheduling the next meeting is very easy. If the person does not jump at the opportunity, don't press the issue, just continue to talk with them as your paths cross. Some people are not as aggressive as others in their efforts to grow their network, and others do not like to do so at all. Become good at reading other people.

When you do meet with someone for coffee or lunch, keep it casual. Save elaborate meals for clients and instead, go to your local coffee house or casual lunch spot. Let the other person pick the place if possible. Even if you do the inviting and plan to pay, when you agree on a date and time ask "Where would be a convenient place for you?" If someone has to drive across town to meet with you, you run a greater risk of their canceling than if you meet at the restaurant next to their office.

Some people try to invite new contacts to golf or other outings that require a large time investment. Generally, people are not willing to set aside four hours or more for someone when there is no mutually beneficial established connection. To slot someone into a "bigger" event before you know them well enough could cause them to refuse the invitation, and limit your chance to advance the friendship.

One reason that you want to be continuously meeting new people is that you will need to be sure that you always have a pool of people to call on. If your network is small, you will have a lot of downtime in your networking efforts. If you have an extensive number of contacts, you can always fill your calendar with breakfast, lunch or coffee meetings with key contacts.

First impressions

A first impression can be so powerful that it can be the difference between having a chance to grow the relationship further and being immediately written off.

Here are three things to keep in mind when you're meeting people for the first time:

Appearance. People expect you to have a certain amount of professionalism in your appearance. While a personal style is good, make sure that your appearance fits within the standards for industry. If there's any doubt, there are articles, books and image consultants who can assist you in making the correct wardrobe choices.

As with so many things, knowing your audience is imperative. If you, as a man, will be attending an event where most people will be coming straight from the office, you will be out of place in a casual pair of pants and a golf shirt. It's smarter to be better dressed. Slacks are a better choice than khakis. In addition, even if others are wearing polo-style shirts, a crisp dress shirt still has a more professional look and feel. For women, a pants suit is appropriate nearly everywhere. There are some professions where skirts or dresses are *de rigeur* and if you're in one of those fields, chances are you know it. When in doubt, dress up.

The firm handshake. In the United States it is customary to shake someone's hand when you meet them. Unless you are a famous germaphobe, like Donald Trump, most people will expect a handshake. A handshake can express confidence or lack thereof. When the appropriate time arrives for a handshake, extend your hand so that the web between your thumb and forefinger presses to the same part of their hand. Firmly clasp your hand to theirs and shake, while maintaining eye contact.

Eye contact. Making then maintaining eye contact with the person you are talking to is critical. By looking someone in the eyes you are showing them that you are interested in what they have to say. You are also showing them that you are fully present in the conversation.

"In talking with people, you don't begin by discussing the things on which you differ. Begin by emphasizing - and keep on emphasizing - the things on which you agree." [5]

—Dale Carnegie

One final point on first impressions: many people get so excited when they meet a potential client that they immediately jump into "selling mode." They instantly try to tell the person everything they can about why they should be doing business together. This is the definition of pushy. In any business that involves relationship selling, the first time you meet someone is not the right time to sell to them. If they are really that good of a prospect, you should be patient and talk to them about things other than just what you do for a living. It is better to find other areas where you have common interests and begin to build the friendship. In a true business relationship, there will be plenty of time to sell them your product or service.

Who Buys?

In a networking situation, it's commonplace for the person who does the inviting to pick up the check. If the person who pays says "you can get it next time," this sets the tone for the give and take nature of any future relationship, and,

---

5 Dale Carnegie, *How to Win Friends and Influence People* (Pocket, revised edition 1981), page 152

if there really is a connection, assumes that you will get together again.

Thom's System:
I keep track of whose turn it is to buy by noting it in my database then referring to it before I leave for the lunch, coffee, dinner, etc.

If you do not have a corporate expense account, or if the other person is not someone for whom you can justify expensing the meal, then plan to pay for it out of your own pocket. Having coffee is a good budget-conscious alternative.

Go where the people are

The people you want to meet are out there somewhere. You just have to know where to look. Venues are key. If you want to know CFOs, then attend your local Financial Executives International (FEI) meeting. If dentists are your target market, find a reason to attend a dental conference.

All industries have trade associations and other groups that hold conferences or local luncheons to help educate their members and provide networking opportunities. While some of these groups limit attendance to members, others welcome anyone.

Physically attend the events

Many people join organizations thinking that their membership and a listing in the directory will lead to business. Yet making it a priority to attend the various events takes a commitment.

While speaking to MBA program participants at St. Edward's University, I referenced the importance of making the time for this type of networking. A student raised his hand and asked how one balances the time involved with having to network, which often happens at breakfast meetings, luncheons or after hours, with other commitments. He was concerned with his ability to effectively network since most of the best times to network took place outside of regular work hours and he also had a young family. His concern was legitimate. The reality was, though, that if he thought that knowing people would be beneficial for advancing his career, he needed to find the time.

Thom's System:
I am commonly out in the evenings because of my community involvement. If more than two events take place during a week, I make the decision which ones to skip. While some may think that two nights during the workweek is excessive, it works for my family. Without the time commitment my wife and I agreed upon early in my career, I would not have the job I have today.

Your goal is to meet between three to five new people at every event you attend. That's ambitious considering that you must also talk to all the people there you already know to keep those relationships going. The best way to accomplish both is to function as a connector, a person who actively tries to introduce people to others. This enables you to network and cultivate existing relationships at the same time. It takes practice to make this not seem forced but it is an incredibly valuable, time-saving strategy.

Speaking at events makes you the expert

Being the keynote speaker at a conference or delivering a break-out seminar is a great way to become known, as long as you have something to say and can be entertaining in your presentation. Above-average public speakers instantly establish themselves as experts. People are always taken with those who can deliver a successful presentation.

What is the definition of an expert? Someone from out of town. This seems to be even more true of those who present at luncheons and conferences. Even if you only focus on increasing your visibility at a local level, being able to speak well will give you an advantage. Organizations are always looking for people to moderate panels or deliver informative presentations at their meetings. While it takes a lot of practice and effort, becoming known as someone who can speak well will lead to many networking opportunities.

Take Aways:

1. Develop, polish then use your elevator pitch.

2. Treat everyone with respect.

3. Reach out to people you have a connection with.

5

SOCIAL NETWORKING

Since the arrival of the Internet in our daily lives, people have communicated and made connections with others around the world via email, bulletin boards, chat rooms and online social networking services. Where the term "networking" could once only apply to building and cultivating connections with those whom you could meet in person or over the telephone, almost everyone on the planet is now within reach.

What is Social Networking?

There are many ways that people can find each other online, but the huge rise in the social networking sites has received a lot of attention from individual subscribers, investors and the media. MySpace, LinkedIn, Friendster, Ryze, ecademy.com, Hoovers Connect and others have popped up offering people the chance to make, grow and keep their business relationships.

In 2006 Rupert Murdoch's News Corp. purchased MySpace for $580 million. The MySpace phenomenon took hold with teenagers and college students, but is also heavily used by business professionals to create virtual brochures about themselves in an effort to reach others who share similar interests. By being a member you can join and create online communities that meet your individual needs.

Here are some common uses for networking sites:

- Friends who want to chat online

- Single people who want to meet other singles

- Amateur matchmakers who want to connect their friends with other friends

- Families who want to keep in touch and map their family trees

- Business people and co-workers interested in networking

- Classmates and study partners

- People looking for long lost friends

Some sites, such as LinkedIn, focus only on the needs of business professionals looking to network, sell their products and services, find a new job, or recruit employees.

Posting a profile on these services is usually free, but many have higher levels of membership that offer advanced levels of usage for a fee.

Why is it important to you?

As with anything that is popular, you need to know what tools others are using. Even if you are not actively using online social networking sites for your own contacts, you want to have a basic understanding of their services and who is using them. Open an account on one of them so that you have an online presence. You will be surprised how many people you already know will discover your profile and send you invitations to join their networks.

Social networking sites are a great tool for finding former business colleagues, and as more and more people join in, it becomes a fast way to search for and reconnect with those whom you have lost touch. When I was asked to be linked to a college fraternity brother via LinkedIn, I discovered that his network included dozens of old friends. It was great to be able to exchange emails with them and learn about their lives and careers two decades later. Many had jobs in industries that were complementary to mine, and by reconnecting I could also tap into future business opportunities.

The Benefits of Social Networking

The professional benefits of these online networking sites can be many if their membership includes the demographics of those with whom you wish to connect. However, like any community, you have to invest time to understand the protocol and proper etiquette of how to interact within the site. And each social networking site is a little different.

Contact management

Social networking communities can make it easier for you to regularly review your contacts and view their current career status. People change jobs often and it is easy to lose touch with people when their email address and phone numbers change. If they keep their online profile up to date then you will instantly have access to their new information. Some sites even offer functionality that alerts you when your contacts update their profiles.

These sites also make it simple for you to see who your contacts are connected with. Sometimes these connections are kept private, but often they are viewable. By regularly reviewing the lists of who your friends are connected to, you can identify business professionals which you'd like to meet and know whom can make the introduction. The process also works in reverse; if there is an individual you are looking to meet, you can trace the connection path back to your network. Often times you will be surprised that the one person who can make the important introduction is someone you regularly speak with.

Found you

Your public profile on these popular websites makes it extremely easy for other people to locate you. When you are looking to expand you network or keep in touch with important contacts, it is necessary that you make it easy for people to locate your contact information. If you hide your profile on the Internet, you might miss valuable opportunities.

Recruiters also use these tools to find candidates for job openings. Always call recruiters back, even if you are not interested in the opportunity. Recruiters can be amazing contacts for you, and for others in your network. Just because you are not interested in a career change today, that may not be the case in a few years. Be excited when you return the call and listen to what they have to say. If you are not interested, let them know, but always find out the complete details of the job they are trying to fill. You might know someone who would be an ideal fit, and both the recruiter and the other person would benefit from your making an introduction.

If you fail to have the common courtesy of returning their phone call, they may overlook you in the future. Additionally, it's a good practice to ask the recruiter questions about the focus of their business and let them know that you would be willing to help them make connections for any future searches that they are working on. If they live in your same town, invite them to join you for coffee or lunch.

My friend Dave Harap is a partner with one of the world's largest employee placement firms. While his practice is both national and international, he is always open to meeting people in his local market. The more contacts he has in a variety of industries, the more valuable he is to his clients. Having strong relationships with recruiters makes you more valuable to your network as well. You never know when you can help someone make that connection.

Successful recruiters are savvy networkers. Their jobs depend on it.

Expanding your geographic reach

Online networking is an incredibly valuable tool when you do business outside your immediate vicinity. Try looking for people you want to know in the city you will be visiting and use your online social network to get advance introductions to key individuals in that city.

Before arriving, schedule coffee, lunch and dinners with new people so that you can build your network on a national or even international basis. By planning ahead, you can keep your calendar full while traveling and maximize your networking opportunities.

Thom's System:
About once a month I will click through my contacts on LinkedIn or Ecademy and review the lists of their contacts to see if there is anyone I would like to meet. I select one or two people that I would like to know and then I call my contact and strategize the best way to obtain an introduction. I do not rely on simply asking for an email introduction, as I realize that everyone is different, and talking with the mutual friend in advance helps to create a more meaningful and appropriate connection.

Caveats

Online networking is not the same as face-to-face networking. Adding someone to your online community does not make them your "instant friend." Real friendships are developed over time and require both the discovery of mutual interests and shared experiences. Many people who do not enjoy the whole concept of networking will often look to these sites as the magic bullet to building relationships. They look at their number of contacts and feel confident that they are doing a good job of creating a network. This may or may not be the case.

Just because you have a digital link does not mean that the other person will have your best interest at heart. It is very difficult to know someone by reading his or her profile. Working in the same industry or having similar interests is not enough for the basis of a strong, mutually beneficial business relationship.

Time Constraints

Maintaining a large online social network can take a huge amount of time. Some people are "link collectors" and will never contact you. Others will inundate you with email. To some folks, having a digital link means that they will send you email on any number of subjects. Since you do not know them personally, their messages will most likely just become more spam that will clutter your inbox.

Some people in the online networking world view the quantity of connections as the important element. These people will invite hundreds (if not thousands) of people to join their networks without ever having met them. Give some thought to whether you wish to connect to those you have not personally met or have online relationships with. When I speak to businesses on the topic of networking I will often get invitations to join the network of those in the audience. It is my belief that having lots of links to those that you do not really know dilutes the power of your network.

Since members in these online communities are not pre-screened or educated on the purpose of the service, you have no way of knowing the goals of people whom you might encounter. Just because someone has a profile on one of these sites does not mean they welcome everyone on the planet to contact them. Just as when you meet someone at a face-to-face event, you need to follow properly the steps to begin a conversation. Do not assume you have the right to call on them because you stumbled upon them online.

Take Aways:

1. *Embrace online social networking as an important tool to help build your network.*

2. *Keep your profiles and contact information up to date so others can find you.*

3. *Only link to those whom you actually know.*

6

YOUR TOOLBOX:

TRICKS OF THE TRADE

While this book focuses on the value an active network brings, a strong product or service offering is also part of the equation. Remember, all things being equal, people will do business with people they know and like. This assumes that you have an apples to apples comparison with what they are purchasing. Jeff Wells, who is shopping for luxury car, will not buy a Hyundai just because his next door neighbor owns the local Hyundai dealership. But if the two local BMW dealers offer Jeff nearly the same price for the same car, he will purchase it from the dealer he likes best. Call it intuition, trust or just plain 'ole charisma, they will always buy from the person to whom they feel a stronger connection.

The Basics

People often neglect basic etiquette when networking. Scott Ingram at NetworkInAustin.com shared with me the following guidelines for networking:

- Use the words "please" and "thank you" frequently

- Arrive at appointments on time, preferably early

- Call if you're running late

- Ignore your cell phone or better yet, turn it off

- Don't take anyone for granted

- Do what you say you're going to do

- Apologize if you screw up

We all get busy and caught up in our own stuff. This can make it easy to forget about others' feelings. I am amazed by how often people will cancel a lunch meeting at the last minute by saying that "something suddenly came up." Do you remember this episode on the Brady Bunch? Translation: Something more important than *you* has come up.

Appointments are important to both parties. Once you have put a meeting on your calendar, and then someone else wants that time slot, do not judge which is more important. Keep your original commitment and suggest another time to the second person. Use common sense, too. If you're a quota-carrying salesperson, lunches probably aren't your best bet during the last few days of the month.

Sometimes things pop up that are out of your control, like having to attend a conference out of town, your child's school holiday performance, etc. But these are exceptions. In general, you can control your own calendar.

Never Confuse Visibility with Credibility

Many people become well known and well liked but without the experience and right product offering, then they will not see the benefit. It doesn't mean that they have wasted their time; if they are industrious then they will one day be able to use those connections to their advantage. Sometimes, however, people try to fool others and position themselves or their company as something they are not. In that case their credibility and reputation will be damaged.

"Adam" arrived in town with claims of having raised a lot of money to launch a company in a particularly hot niche. He tried to build a network of as many influential people as he could in short order. He asked people he met to make more introductions, and would drop names of his new "friends" to gain meetings with even more important people. He was often quoted in the media and, in turn, hired some ambitious young people to work for him. These people told everyone how great his company was and how they were making such a difference in the community.

But Adam lacked the funding that he claimed. His employees found their paychecks bouncing, the rent went unpaid and the folks in the local business community realized that he was telling all of them the same thing and using their names to help build his network. There was "no there, there."

Eventually the word on the street was that Adam was a fraud and people whispered warnings to each other to steer clear of him. Adam's company closed its doors and he left town just as fast as he arrived. While he had gained a lot of visibility in six months, there was no credibility to back it up. Two years later, almost no one remembers Adam.

And then there is "Phil." Shortly after Phil came to town because of a job transfer, he began to meet people in the local business community. He cautiously asked people about the important organizations for young entrepreneurial professionals. He never abused any confidences and slowly began to make friends. He volunteered with a local charity and became one of its board members. A year after his arrival he decided to found a new company. He had a track record of success and had developed a good reputation so it was easy for him to partner with other companies and quickly bring on clients. While he was building the new company he continued to network, make introductions, and volunteer his time. Over time he has developed the reputation for being a successful businessman who now employs over one hundred people, and has won numerous business and civic awards. He knows most of the important people in town and is sought after for his counsel regularly. He is both visible and credible.

Visibility alone will get you nothing, and eventually people will see through your façade. To be famous without substance is useless in business.

Stand Up and Be Heard

Public speaking is often cited as the number one most feared thing by Americans. Death ranks number two. If this rings a bell, I have two words for you: Toastmasters International.

I have been an active member of Toastmasters for 15 years and am still amazed by how many people have never heard of the organization, which has been around since 1924. Its charter reads: "Through participation in the Toastmasters Communication and Leadership Program, people from all backgrounds learn to effectively speak, conduct a meeting, manage a department or business, lead, delegate, and motivate." These are all skills that can help you in business.

There are Toastmasters clubs in every major US metropolitan area and in 80 countries. Many people who are familiar with the organization have never looked into it because they think the clubs are made up of only advanced speakers. To begin with, you will benefit from enhancing your public speaking skills, regardless of your industry of job function. Clubs are made up of people with a variety of speaking skills. Joining Toastmasters is the smartest career move I have made. I have had countless experiences where I have been called upon to address a crowd, formally or informally, and I never could have succeeded in such talks without the skills that I have fine-tuned through Toastmasters.

In addition, many people have actually made business connections from people they have met within Toastmasters. People have met future employers and employees because they are exposed to people who are focused on personal growth, and often find like-minded others.

You can find all the information you need at www.toastmaster.org.

Toastmasters International
PO Box 9052
Mission Viejo, CA 92690
USA
Tel: (949) 858-8255

Treat Everyone with Respect

You are busy. Time seems to be the one commodity you can never quite get your hands around. You need to spend your time talking to people who can lead to business and yet you are constantly being barraged by people who do nothing but waste your time. If this is how you approach networking, you have missed the point: it is not all about you! Look to make connections with people that you like and that have a similar, mutually beneficial attitude toward helping others. Most people have to work at this because it is easy to fall into the habit of deciding if people are "important" enough for your precious time and effort. While everyone would like to know just the movers and shakers, that is not how the real world operates.

When I sold financial printing for RR Donnelley, my success was dependent on relationships with the top corporate and securities attorneys in my town. These lawyers influenced which financial printer their clients selected so knowing them was imperative. Yet the most successful partners were also the busiest and thus, the hardest to reach. Many people would have focused on meeting the partners and ignored everyone else. To force a friendship on these lawyers would not have worked because they did not know who I was, nor did they care. Instead, I concentrated on those around them, the ones who were generally overlooked by my competitors. I used my connections from the American Marketing Association to meet the marketing managers for the firms and developed relationships with them, later on asking for introductions to their top attorneys.

Face time

While at networking events, work hard to remain actively involved in the conversation you are currently engaged in. More times than not, people who are engaged in one conversation are scanning the room to see who else is present. Once they spot that "better" person, they abruptly end the conversation and run off to talk to that other individual. While it's important to circulate and talk to as many people as possible, how you conduct yourself in the present is part of the impression you will leave behind.

Learning how to end conversations gracefully is an art. If you want to end a conversation, there are several polite ways to move on without being abrupt. Acknowledge the other person's comments and tell them that you look forward to talking with them more in the future. Another strategy is to tell the other person that you do not want to monopolize all of their time at the event, as you know there are many others that they want to speak with. You have put the focus on them and avoid being rude.

"Darrin" was highly regarded by mutual friends yet whenever our paths crossed, he was less than cordial. Then I began working for a law firm and Darrin, whose business offering was consulting services to law firms, suddenly wanted to get to know me. He failed to remember that you never know where someone will end up. More amazing was that when I first met him, my primary clients were partners in law firms. By the time my value was obvious to Darrin, I had already established a negative opinion of him, and would not have recommended him under any circumstance.

The Hard Goods

When you are committed to successfully creating a network of contacts that can and will lead to more business and a successful career path, much of your effort will be in the intangible art of relationship building. There are a few things you can do to help make a good first impression.

Business Cards

Your business card is your most important networking tool. Once you have met someone and decide that you want to get to know them better, you need to get their business card so that you can easily access their pertinent information. Carry your business cards with you at all times. Steve, a financial planner, exchanged business cards with someone he met in his local hospital's Emergency Room waiting area, where they were both waiting to be seen. This exchange turned into new business.

Here are a few pointers for those of you who have input into the design of your business cards:

✓ Do have a professional look to your cards. While you can purchase inexpensive cards online or print them on your laser printer, if you go cheap, you will look cheap. The card is part of your image. Card stock is a must.

✓ Do print lots of them. Some employers issue very few cards and encourage their employees to ration them. Cards, even high-quality cards, are relatively inexpensive.

✓ Do enclose business cards in your correspondence. Of course there does come a point where you can overdo this, so use your best judgment. Early in my career I had a prospective client tell me that, after a year of receiving marketing materials from me, she had collected a whole box of my cards. While she said this jokingly, I got the message.

✓ Do use a color logo on your card. Years ago, having color on your business card was cost prohibitive. Today color is inexpensive.

✓ Do be sure your email address is on your card.

✓ Do be brief. Your business card is not your resumé or a marketing brochure. If you do a good job of networking and making connections, your name and company should be enough to trigger a reminder about what you discussed when you met.

✓ Do go with the standard business card size and shape. Unusually shaped cards are difficult to place in a wallet or card case, and thus might not make it back to the recipient's office, which means your contact information is lost.

✓ Do have a light color or even white on the reverse side of your card. While color is good, you want to be sure that people can jot notes on it if they wish.

Nametags

When attending a business event, knowing someone's first name and the company they work for is an easy conversation opener. A conversation can easily begin with "Hi Bill, I know someone who works for Bank of America… ," or "Mary, I have not heard of The Hill Group. What does your company do?" Many times people either do not wear nametags (or, frighteningly, the organization hosting the event does not provide them) or the text is too small for the average person to read. The most common mistake of all occurs when people have to write their own nametag: it's illegible. People with less than perfect penmanship need to make sure that it's clear and it's neat.

Be sure to put your first and last name and, under that, your company name. Some people shy away from writing the company name or put it in code. The law firm Andrews Kurth is referred to internally as AK. If an attorney writes "AK" on his or her nametag at a public event, people will not understand. However, when a company is branded by its initials—IBM and 3M are good examples of this—it is not only acceptable, it is preferred.

One final point about nametags: wear them where they can be seen. This does not mean on your belt or in another obscure but visible location. Nametags make it easy for others to learn your name and your company affiliation. Let your nametag do its job.

Stationery

High-quality, personalized note cards are worth the investment. I have some inexpensive yet very nice fold-over cards with my name printed on the front. I have always used these (and paid for them myself) rather than use ones that have my employer's logo on them, because connecting with people is personal, not a corporate, function. No matter how much companies try to believe that customers have relationships with the business, the truth is that the relationship rests with the individuals who represent the business. I do, however, always include a business card in my correspondence so the company name and logo are part of the interaction.

Finally, always write in pen. I once received a note written on inexpensive paper and in pencil. While the follow-up was appreciated, it was hard to take it seriously.

Knowledge is Power

It's not what you know, it's whom you know. While this is true, it is not the whole truth. Whom you know is important and the more you know, the better. Not only must you be knowledgeable about your industry and the general business climate, but the more background you have about the people you interact with, the more power you have in cultivating a strong personal relationship.

This is information in the positive sense. The more you know about a person, the easier it is to build a connection. The more tidbits that you grasp, the better the chance that you will find common ground from which to launch in-depth conversations and discover things about each other that become the foundation of a friendship.

Taking a genuine interest in people makes you a more effective networker. Recalling someone's past experiences, their interests, their careers and their families will help you stand out from the crowd. Have you ever run into someone whom you have not seen in a long time and they ask you specific things about your kids, pets or co-workers? It's impressive when people remember the details of your life and it sends a clear message that they were listening to you the previous time you met. Unfortunately this won't happen on its own; you need to make an effort to gather information about people and find a way to track and easily recall it.

Memory Tricks

When you are actively networking and meeting new people, on occasion you will have trouble remembering people's names. To avoid this problem, learn some memory tricks that will help you remember names. Here are a few basic tips to get you started:

Repeat the person's name out loud after or introduce them to someone else. Using their name in conversation may help you recall their name later. You can also invent a relationship in your mind between their name and their physical characteristics. One example for Shirley Temple could be "her curly (rhymes with Shirley) hair is cut short near her temples."

Always get a business card. Getting the other person's business card is a tool to help you remember them.

Add people to your database. Regardless of which kind of system you use to keep track of your contacts, be sure to regularly add new people into your database.

Thom's System:
I make it a point to review my database and notes on business cards on a regular basis. I try to go over the information at least once a month in order to keep it fresh in my mind. This exercise also triggers me to contact people whom I have not spoken to in a while.

Talk about people whom you have recently met. By sharing information with others, it will help your memory. In addition, others you work with will now know about the people you have met.

Jane, a popular business speaker avoids saying "nice to meet you" when she is introduced to people. Over the years Jane has met thousands of people at events where she has spoken and, since she was the expert, these people all remember her. Often "nice to meet you" is met with "oh, we have met before...". Jane has found that "nice to see you" works better. However, if you are introduced to someone who obviously knows you, and you have not the foggiest idea of who they are, it is generally best to own up to it and admit that you do not remember them. If you handle it correctly, it can be a lot better than pretending you know them.

Keeping your facts straight

If you rely on a computer then you should also rely on Customer Relationship Management (CRM) software. This can range from simple shareware to a customized, expensive solution. Regardless, you must have some kind of database where you can easily store and access information. In years past the Rolodex was the gold standard. Today you are more than likely have that information on your computer and/or your portable handheld device, and have the ability to store much more information, including photographs, links to websites and articles.

The more information, the better

Sometimes you come across information in roundabout ways, and while you may have no immediate need for it, if you don't record it, it will be lost to you later.

I once discovered the birthday of a client quite by accident. My wife ran into his wife at a local department store. In conversation, my client's wife said that she was shopping for her husband's birthday gift, and made mention that the big day was the following Tuesday. My wife relayed this information to me and I promptly input it into my database and sent a card. Every year after that I sent a card to his office. Recently he called to thank me for the annual card, and he inquired how I even knew when his birthday was.

In addition to birthdays, anniversaries, spouses and children's names, note where a person grew up, went to high school and college, former places they have worked, etc. For example, if you know that someone attended San Diego State University, and you know their approximate age, you can talk about Marshall Faulk and be pretty sure to have a topic of conversation if they're sports-minded. (Faulk was one of the few true NFL superstars to emerge from the San Diego State Aztec football team). In addition, knowing someone attended college at Duke may give you a reason to take them to dinner and a college basketball game if Duke is coming to town to play your home team. Knowledge of someone's hobbies will always give you something to talk about or give you a way to find a unique gift. Imagine that one of your prospects is an avid fly fisherman. Even though you have no interest or knowledge in fly fishing, you can start a conversation with "I understand you love fly fishing; how did you get involved in that?" It's likely that your companion will be happy to tell you about his experiences. People like to talk about things that interest them, and even if you do not have any knowledge of the topic, they are often happy to explain it to you.

Take Aways:

1. *You need both visibility and credibility.*

2. *Develop strong pubic speaking skills.*

3. *The more you know about the people in your network, the better.*

7

BUILD A BETTER MOUSETRAP:

BE CREATIVE

It's easy to just follow the leader. You see this in advertising all the time; companies advertise where their competition advertises, assuming that it's bringing the other company success. While it takes more brainpower to stand apart from the crowd, it's a better strategy. After all, new ideas get more attention.

Make it Memorable

The KT Company was considering kiosk advertising in the local airport. Their largest competitor did this and several of KT's senior executives were convinced that they were missing out on a lot of potential business because they did not have this exposure. Every time one of them got on or off an airplane they saw their competitor's advertisement. They then jumped to the conclusion that every business-person in the city was having the same reaction, and therefore the competitor's telephone must be ringing off the hook. The fact that they were pre-conditioned to notice the competition was lost on them. To the average business traveler, their competitor's ad was just one of many.

Do more than a holiday card

Consider your company's holiday card. How many of the cards you received last year were not even signed or addressed by hand? The computer has been a great tool for streamlining the process, but a foil-stamped signature on the inside and a laser printed label is hardly a warm and fuzzy greeting of the season.

Don't stop sending holiday cards or abandon all activities that are common for companies in your industry. It's even worse to be noticed by your absence. Expand your activities beyond the predictable. Find a way to reach out to your clients on a monthly or quarterly basis.

Do you need an occasion?

While you can use a less traditional holiday to make contact, you can also do it "just because." Try picking one day each month to write short notes to clients and members of your network just to let them know that you're thinking about them. If you send 10 such cards a month, over the course of a year you would personally reach out to 120 people.

Send articles

In your dealings with people, you will learn both about things that are important to their business, and about their personal interests. During your regular current events and industry reading, make a habit of clipping or photocopying articles that are of interest to people in your network. If the article is online, email them a link with a note that simply says, "Thought you would enjoy this article." People are flattered by the personal attention. Be sure not to forward mass email links of an article to your whole database, as that does not show any personal thought and is, instead, annoying.

Another good habit is to flag articles whose authors are in your network. Send them a handwritten note with the original article or send them an email telling them that you read their article. If appropriate, compliment them on a job well done, and share with them why you found the article relevant. While individuals write for a variety of reasons, everyone likes to know that someone read their work and appreciated it. You can even use this technique with people you don't know and you will be surprised how often people will thank you for taking the time to contact them.

Functional Functions

Participating in organized business events or creating memorable business functions is a great way to have direct interaction with potential clients and others who can become important referral sources. People who are savvy in network building go out of their way to participate in or host events.

Client Parties

During the high-tech boom of the 90s it was typical for companies to host extravagant parties; the frequency of these events made them seem commonplace. With the sluggish economy we've seen since the bust, these parties are all but obsolete.

Still, bringing people together for a nice event goes a long way. However, nothing is worse than hosting a big event and then not having anyone show up. If you have never hosted a large client party in the past, there may not be a compelling reason for the people you invite to attend; to successfully execute a large-scale client event takes the participation of the management team and others who have strong ties outside the company. In addition to sending an invitation and a "save the date" notification, people will need to phone those in their networks and encourage them to attend. These kinds of calls have a powerful effect in getting people to actually show up at an event.

Sporting Events

One of the age-old ways to bond with other business people is through sports. Golf has long been a staple of client entertaining because people who enjoy golf are thrilled to get out of the office to play. The fact that it's a scenic, quiet game lends itself to conversation.

Big companies may also have tickets or luxury box suites for their local professional sports. While the cost of these tickets is high, if used correctly they can have great impact on building relationships. Think long and hard about giving these tickets away without attending with the client or prospect. Many a person believes they are doing something great by handing tickets to a basketball game to someone they are trying to build a relationship with. When you give someone tickets to a sporting event they have an experience. When you attend with them, you *share* in that experience. Which will bring you more benefit in the end?

Be careful about giving tickets away. "Steve" had long been trying to get to know a particular prospect. One day he got a call from the prospect saying he desperately wanted two tickets to the Rose Bowl and was hoping that Steve could help him out. He quickly purchased four tickets and gave the prospect the other two, neglecting to mention that he would be seated next to him. When he arrived at the game, he found the prospect's 15-year-old son and his buddy in the two seats. Meanwhile, the prospect was seated across the stadium, with the competitor. Giving away tickets does not buy appreciation. It's better to only use the firm's tickets as a way to build the relationship by making the game into a shared outing.

Small Gatherings

When it comes to networking, the fallacy exists that bigger events are better. Yet it is not about how many people you can stand in the room with, it is about how you can make connection with. "Piggy Back" events can be a good choice. If another company is hosting a cocktail party from 6:00 p.m. – 8:00 p.m., this is a great opportunity to plan a dinner at a nearby restaurant starting at 8:30 p.m. It is best to call and invite some guests who you know will be at the main event. That way they will know in advance that they will be out later that evening. Also, they will inevitably tell others that they were invited to dinner with you. Be sure to save a couple of seats for people you meet at the event and wish to invite along. If you have eight people going to dinner, make your reservation for 10 or 12. It is easier for the restaurant to make your table smaller than to add two people at the last minute.

Whenever you are planning to attend an industry conference, check the schedule in advance to see if there is a night when there is no official event planned. But don't wait until the last minute, as others will inevitably be hosting dinners as well.

You can also do an "After Party." If there is an awards dinner or other event in your community that is well attended, you can be the one who keeps the party going. In Austin, Ernst & Young's Entrepreneur of the Year Awards is the biggest event in the local business community. After the ceremony ends, the party continues into the wee hours of the morning. One of my former employers annually hosts the After Party, which includes a band, cigars and plenty of networking opportunities. How exactly did this come about? It started small and informally. The first year a few clients and friends were taken out for drinks after the awards. The next year the company sent out invitations. The following year they added a band. More than a decade later it is a well-known annual event that is as much a part of the evening as the awards themselves.

Unique Ways to Stand Out

Sometimes people are afraid to try new things in a business situation. Following are some event ideas that gave the host the chance to build a relationship with others, and also be remembered.

My friend Dave frequently entertains for business. Because he deals in six figures, his clients and prospects are used to being wined and dined. Dave has developed a trademark dining style. Once the group is seated he asks for an order or two of the restaurant's signature dessert to be served as an appetizer, with as many forks as people at the table. It is unexpected and something that, while most people enjoy, everyone comments on. From time to time I meet people who also know Dave and they never fail to ask me "Have you ever been to dinner with him when he orders dessert first?" Dave will always be remembered for this gesture.

Another friend, an avid reader, frequently sends people books that they have discussed during their meeting. While the content of the book itself is important, the gesture of recalling the conversation, recognizing the person's interests and needs, and taking action after the meeting is more important.

Did you know that you can rent a major league ballpark for batting practice? Bobby attended such an event at AT&T Park, where the San Francisco Giants play.

The team's coaches hit pop flies to the outfield and grounders to the infield, and the attendees also got a chance to bat. Bars were set up in the dugouts and the usual stadium vendors walked around with peanuts and popcorn. Years later, Bobby still talks about it.

> *"Stock your library with extra copies of your favorite books. It's hard to beat the gift of a book, especially right after a meeting."* [6]
>
> —*Tim Sanders*

Child's Play

Many of my clients have young children. One spring I bought a block of tickets to a baseball game and invited along some clients and prospects and their four-year-olds. My daughter and I hosted the kids and their dads for an evening at the ballpark. For most of the kids, this was their first baseball game. For the dads it was a chance to mix business with parenting, something they had not likely done before. It was a good networking event for all the dads, and a great opportunity for me to stand out. One guy even pointed out that in all his years in business, he had plenty of chances to invite his wife along to events, but never before had he been invited to bring his son.

---

6 Tim Sanders, *Love is the Killer App: How to Win Business and Influence Friends,* (Crown Business, 2002) page 91

Another twist on the event with kids concept is what was done by the Austin office of a large law firm. When Happy Feet was released in 2006, the firm invited its prospects, clients and other friends to bring their children and join them for a Sunday afternoon screening. They provided stuffed toys of the movie's main character cleverly branded wearing a law-firm-logo'd t-shirt for every kid, took photos of each family with a life-sized penguin which they personally emailed to everyone later in the week, and opened up the concession stands hosted-bar style. My own kids were duly impressed.

The Best Business Relationships are Personal

Some people argue that you should keep your business life business and your personal life personal. They do not think it to be a good career move to become too close to their clients and co-workers. Although people who feel this way seem to be few and far between, you will encounter people who are steadfast in their theory that they have "enough friends," and will give you push back if you try to make connections with them on a more familiar level. If you do encounter these individuals, be respectful and interact with them in a very courteous and professional manner. However, if you are above average at relationship-building skills, you will find that even these folks will come around with time.

So, if given the chance to be all business or forge friendships that can either last a lifetime or that can come and go throughout your lifetime, strive to have some level of connection that leaves behind a positive impression.

More examples of the personal touch:

- You discover that someone you network with enjoys wine so you send them an unusual bottle. If you lack wine knowledge, your local wine store will happily educate you and make recommendations. My college roommate frequents a small winery near his home in the Napa Valley. He buys cases of wine and the vintner signs the bottles with messages such as "Happy Birthday" or "Congratulations." Since the winery's name bears the vintner's name, it makes for a great gift. How many of your clients do you think have ever received a bottle of wine with the personal signature of the vintner?

- Do you know someone who is a big sports fan? Invite them to join your fantasy football league. If your colleges happen to play each other, place a friendly wager, with the winner sending the loser a bottle of wine. Acknowledge the fact that they made it to the national championships, or replaced their coach.

- Send baby gifts. Cookie bouquets stand out. So do personalized gifts. You will usually remember the child's name if you order a personalized gift, too!

- When someone gets a new job, acknowledge the event, be it a promotion or firm change. A card or an email works well, but an invitation to a celebratory lunch is even better and it gives you a legitimate reason to spend time together.

- When someone you know well has their first article published you can have it framed for them. Any local frame or craft store can do this for under $50 and it makes a huge impression. Hanging on my office wall is an article I wrote for the *Austin Business Journal*. It's an uncommon gift and one that I have only received once in my career.

- When someone you know writes a book, buy a case to give as gifts. When my wife published her first cookbook, *Mad at Martha*, a friend of ours bought copies for his clients as holiday presents. He had traditionally given his clients a book and this time he was able to have them all personally autographed. In addition, it makes the gift more special when you can tell the recipient "My good friend wrote this. I hope you enjoy it."

- Happy Hour. Host a gathering at a local restaurant or bar with or without a short, relevant speaker. You can also host a wine tasting event in your home. A professional sommelier can come to your house and give a brief presentation. In addition, people often feel a closer connection to people after they have been invited to their home.

Take Aways:

1. Become known for thoughtful, memorable gestures and unique events.

2. Acknowledge those who write articles and also send articles of interest to those in your network.

3. The best business relationships are personal.

8

YOUR PUNCH LIST:

REASONS TO KEEP IN TOUCH

Remaining visible and continually making new connections takes an incredible commitment, one that most people are not willing to make. Those who do find that it is a never-ending cycle; there are always more people to meet.

Continue to Cultivate

Critics liken networking to having a second full-time job, claiming that if they devoted the time to this, they wouldn't have time to do their primary job. In actuality, just the opposite is true. The better connected someone is, the easier they will find their job.

Even if you master the steps of making people part of your network, you cannot neglect the final, most important step: maintaining those relationships. Once you have established true connections with people, you still need to invest the time to keep them going.

Everyone has had important people in their lives with whom they have lost contact. To keep any relationship thriving takes an active "give and take." In a business setting, letting a relationship become stale opens the door for the competition.

"Relationships are the result of effort. Unless you are willing to accept that, you won't create positive ripples or build productive relationships." [7]

—Steve Harper

Have a significant "touch point" every quarter

If you only have a small network, keeping in touch can be an easy thing. You will run into people, exchange phone calls or emails, and be able to keep the relationship alive with very little planning and effort. However, as your contact database grows and your clients, prospects and friends expands into the hundreds, it becomes much harder to just let the process happen. You need to find ways to reach large numbers of people at one time without it becoming too impersonal. Here are a few ways you can reach out to your contacts.

One-on-One Meetings. There will never be anything more important than the one-on-one meeting. Regardless of whether it takes place over coffee, lunch, drinks or dinner, spending time with someone and having an uninterrupted dialog is the best way to cultivate a lasting business relationship. However, as your network grows, it becomes impossible to meet with everyone in this type of setting.

7 Steve Harper, *The Ripple Effect* (SWOT Publishing, 2005) page 154

Newsletters. Whether you send a printed newsletter or an electronic version, this can be a great way to relay information to your clients and prospects. However, so many companies now have some form of newsletter that you need to find some reason to get people to read yours. Chad, a local small business owner, has created a monthly newsletter for clients, prospects and friends. In addition to its standard content, it also includes a business trivia quiz on little-known facts about the business community or famous tycoons. Readers can email or call in their answer and on the 15th of each month he has a drawing to award a $100 gift certificate to a local restaurant. He regularly receives more than 150 responses! In the newsletter the following month he prints the answer and the name of the winner. This strategy makes his newsletter stand out.

Seminars. You can reach out to people by inviting them to periodic seminars that your company puts on that can benefit their businesses. Technology firms have done this for a long time but it translates to any business with a product or service offering. These can be large, multi-day events or smaller, more intimate gatherings. If you have presentable office space, these gatherings can take place in your conference room. Bringing people to your place of business helps them feel connected to your company. If you do not have enough space, or your facility is not suitable for outside visitors, alternative meeting space is easy to find. Hotels, private clubs and restaurants often have good meeting spaces, and most cities now have businesses that lease meeting room space at affordable rates.

Regardless of the venue, pay special attention to the quality of the presentation. It is best to have the speaker not be from your company. You can either pay to bring in a recognized expert on the topic or you can partner with another company who will benefit from the exposure. The presenter should be exceptionally skilled because if you plan to do these types of meetings on a regular basis, you need to be sure that the attendees will be impressed with both the content and the delivery.

Other Speaking Opportunities. If you or a prominent individual at your company has a high-profile speaking engagement, use this as an opportunity to reach out to your network. Think about who would benefit from attending the event and invite them to attend as your guest. Include the agenda noting when you will be speaking. If there is a fee, let them know that you will be taking care of it, and that they will be among your special guests. Speakers generally receive a number of free admissions. If the organizer doesn't offer, just ask. People appreciate the invitation to hear someone they know speak.

Public Relations. Another great way to be seen and remembered is to appear in the local press. You can do this by being quoted or writing for them.

Reporters often need expert background information for the stories they are working on and, if they know that you are knowledgeable in your industry, then they will call you for quotes. Keep in mind that a reporter can, and often will, use anything you say in print, so you need to be cautious when being interviewed. However, don't be afraid to talk to reporters; they are just doing their job.

There are countless books on how to talk to the press and companies who specialize in training you and your staff on how to do this. Anyone who is planning to do a lot of interviews should have some formal media training.

Publications often accept articles written by non-staff. Few people actually take the time to author business articles, even though they are relatively easy to write and get published. There are many venues for you to place short business articles: your local business journal, your news daily, your industry publications. Many newsletters and online media are hungry for such articles.

Your firm's public relations agency can manage the placement of these or you can request the publication's editorial guidelines and write to those standards. Additionally, the Internet presents many opportunities to write on topics of interest and value to your client base. Editorial guidelines are available for many of these sites as well.

A published article then becomes a great self-promotion tool. If the article is in print format, you can order reprints from the publisher and use them as part of your marketing materials. Bring them along when you speak at seminars or other events so that people can take a copy with them. Published articles are always a great collateral piece to get into the hands of prospects, clients or friends.

Pay Attention

Times change. You must stay on top of what is happening in and around your network. People will be promoted, leave their jobs to pursue new opportunities, or win industry accolades. People who volunteer their time with non-profits will serve on high-profile boards or receive praise in the press. Their companies will receive press coverage praising their latest product or singling them out for excellence. These are all opportunities for you to continue to build on your relationship with others by acknowledging their accomplishments.

Celebrate the highs

If, while doing your daily reading, you notice that someone in your network has been promoted or won an award, take the time to acknowledge it. Fewer people do this than you would think. It's a nice touch to clip the article and send it along with the note. People are often grateful for extra copies.

On an American Airlines flight I read an article on executive coaching where an acquaintance was quoted. Following my return to the office I sent him an email commenting on some of the more interesting points he had made and mentioned that I still had my copy of the magazine. He responded that, sure enough, he had not yet seen it. You can guess what happened next. It was a great chance to get to know him better that came about all because of a free copy of an airline in-flight magazine.

Another way to celebrate a high is to get three or four others together and take the person to a celebratory lunch at a restaurant. The check can be divisible by the number attending, excepting the honoree, and the individual cost will be minimal while the impact on the honoree will be great.

Support the lows

You also want to be sure to keep up with what is happening in the community economically, because not all news is good news. This includes both business and personal hardships.

Companies go out of business and people lose their jobs. In addition to finding ways to offer your support during rough times, you need to keep abreast of what is happening, as to not embarrass yourself in conversation. Soon after the collapse of Brobeck, Phleger & Harrison, where I had worked for two years, in one of the largest public failures of an international law firm in history, I ran into an acquaintance. After exchanging pleasantries he asked me how things were at Brobeck. It became clear that he had no idea that the firm had dissolved. When I finished bringing him up to date he dug his grave even deeper by saying "funny that it wasn't in the paper." Unfortunately for him, it had been on the front page of all the major news dailies in the country and in most business publications, too.

In addition to business woes, people will have personal crises. When my own infant daughter had to undergo brain surgery at four months of age, some people in my business network reached out while others did not. I am sure that everyone cared, but many said nothing because they weren't sure what to say. Others found ways to make a difference. Three former co-workers gave us airline frequent flier miles to ease the costs associated with seeing specialists in another part of the country. Others brought home-cooked meals to us at home while Kate was recovering. People in our extended network sent flowers and stuffed animals, which filled my daughter's hospital room. And hundreds more sent emails of support and said prayers. All of this made a frightening and stressful experience somewhat easier to handle. And finally, networking also led us from Austin to San Diego to the pediatric neurosurgeon whose new procedure greatly helped my daughter.

No Relationship is Ever Solid Enough

Business is rarely exclusive. If you're in a business without competition and your customers have no choice but to use your services, good for you. For the rest of us, it's not that easy. In *Winning*, Jack Welch writes of a Bank One document he read when involved in the 2004 merger of Bank One and JPMorgan Chase. One of the behaviors in this document is "Communicate daily with your customers. If they are talking to you, they can't be talking to a competitor." [8] It's an interesting thought.

---

8 Jack Welch, *Winning* (HarperBusiness, 2005) page 19

No relationship is bullet proof and even people you think are on your side will sometimes leave you for a competitor. If you take them for granted you can be sure that it will happen, but even if you have done everything right, some will still move on. That's just business. The best way to handle such an event is to keep the relationship active. As easily as they can take their business away, they can bring it back. How you handle the situation can make all the difference in the future.

Client Surveys

Conducting periodic client surveys enables you to quantitatively find out just how well you service your clients. People seem to think that client surveys are bothersome but, in reality, most clients appreciate that you want to improve your service and they can actually help strengthen the relationship, especially if you uncover a concern and act on correcting it.

Here are a few types of surveys:

In Person Surveys. Individual or groups of clients are met with to discuss how your company is performing. The advantage to being in person is that it gives you the chance to directly interact with clients. They can see that you are concerned with how you service them and you can have a nice dialogue. The disadvantage is that people may not give you negative feedback. In addition, if you group clients together, one may bring up a negative point that the others had not yet realized.

Mailed Paper Surveys. This is the most traditional kind of survey. A client can anonymously fill out a questionnaire rating your products and services. The upside is that you can get good information since it's anonymous. The downside is that it is difficult to get people to take the time to fill out these surveys and return them.

Emailed Electronic Surveys. Much like the paper survey, clients can log onto a website and answer a series of questions. The response rate is higher than that of a mailed paper survey, because of the convenience. However, even if anonymity is an option, people may not be fully honest, as they may not believe that their identity is truly confidential.

Third-Party Surveys. Using a third party is advantageous in that they know what kinds of questions to ask so that the feedback can be useful to your organization. Clients may feel more comfortable sharing information with a professional surveyor than with you directly. The downside is cost.

Last thought: To encourage participation you may want to have some kind of a giveaway, a small gift for every participant or a drawing for a larger prize.

Reconnecting

We have all lost contact with people we have known, socially or through business, who have been important to us at various stages of our life. Take a minute and think of a former employer or a college friend who had a positive impact on you. Whatever happened to them? Are they worth tracking down? Could having them back in your life lead to more business, a new job or just put a smile on your face? Reconnecting is an excellent way to help build your network. It's easy because you already have a foundation to build upon and, in many cases, there is no reason that you drifted apart. As should be crystal clear by now, it takes a serious effort to grow and maintain fruitful relationships in the business world. If one or both parties do not invest the time, it is easy to lose people.

Conversely, there may have been a reason that you lost contact: a disagreement or a misunderstanding. If the person has lied, cheated, or has character issues, it is just as well that you no longer interact. However, there are times where a minor incident has created a large chasm between you; if you feel the other person in worth investing the effort, you can at least try to reconnect.

Exactly how do you make contact with someone you have not spoken to in a long time? Just pick up the phone and place the call. Some people think it's awkward to call and say hello after so much time has past. It's not. Most people are thrilled to hear from someone from way back when. A sincere compliment is always a nice opener, too, as long as it's genuine.

If you need help finding their current contact information, you can call directory assistance in the city they live in. An even more thorough way is to use an Internet search engine. Google can often provide you with information that will make reconnecting easier. You can also try a web site like classmates.com.

If you live in the same city, you may just run into someone you've been thinking of reconnecting with. Since so many things happen in business by serendipity, take advantage of those chance meetings. Who came to mind when you started reading this section? Call them right now.

I once issued this same challenge to an investment banker I worked with. He immediately thought of his former business school roommate. They had lost touch over some silly disagreement, and had not spoken in nearly a decade. He knew his former roommate lived locally so I suggested he take his old friend to lunch with no agenda other than reconnecting. He did, and they have again become friends. Chances are that in the future they will have a strong relationship and be able to help each other professionally as well.

Thinning the Ranks

On the flipside of reconnecting is purposely removing someone from your network. As in other areas of your life, maintaining a network of business contacts will require you to encounter difficult people. In most cases you will just be polite when you cross paths. In some cases, however, you will want to purposely remove them from your network. Steer clear of anyone who does not show good character and respect for others, or who is exceptionally challenging to deal with. You cannot afford to be affiliated with those who are viewed as not having good ethics. It is your responsibility to make sure that you have a positive give and take within your network, and if others are not doing their part, you owe it to yourself to move on.

Tread cautiously when removing people from your circle of contacts. If people feel you are ignoring them or treating them poorly, they will share that information with others. Just let them drift away.

Occasionally, because the "drift away" method has not worked, you will have to actually tell someone that you do not wish to continue a professional relationship. Similar to ending a romantic relationship, this is not easy. But, if the other person is really that difficult to deal with, you just may need to tell them that you do not wish to continue the networking relationship. If you do need to confront them, be sure to be as diplomatic and kind as possible. Let them know that you do not feel that you share mutual goals. Most importantly, keep the conversation to yourself. Even in large communities, gossip always finds its way back to the person who is being discussed. The best policy is to not share your personal feelings about anyone.

Take Aways:

1. *Reach out to your clients every quarter.*

2. *Stay up to date on what is happening in your community and with individuals so you can celebrate the highs and support the lows.*

3. *Eliminate people from your network who do not contribute to your relationship.*

9

THE SCAFFOLDING

SUPPORTING YOUR NETWORK:

MENTORS & PEER GROUPS

The road to building a career is a bumpy one. If you are fortunate enough to instinctively know which way turn at every fork in the road and if everyone you meet provides you with excellent advice then you are very lucky. For the rest of us, it's helpful to have some special people whom you can turn to for guidance and maybe some tough love, especially early in your career. These people, mentors, can be invaluable to your long-term success, and help you avoid many of the pitfalls that will come along the way.

What exactly *is* a mentor?

Anyone with more experience than you can be your mentor. They can be older or younger than you, as long as they have more industry knowledge. The relationship can be a formal one where you refer to them as your mentor and have scheduled meetings with specific agendas. Or the relationship can be so informal that neither of you even realizes that they are your mentor. Your mentor is someone whom you regularly turn to for advice, someone who has taken a visible interest in assisting you along the path of your career.

Sometimes a mentor is inside your company. Law firms often assign senior attorneys to work with specific younger lawyers. They teach them how to do their research, introduce them to key people inside the firm and help them chart their path toward partnership. It's easy to see which lawyers had good mentor relationships early in their careers, as they are often the ones who progress the fastest into the partnership and have more successful practices. Often, those who had no mentor or a weak mentor will drift aimlessly and eventually leave the firm.

People often think that a mentor has to be someone from inside your own company or industry. This is untrue. If you are open to having a mentor, it is not difficult to find an individual who will take an interest in your career and offer helpful advice along the way. You can meet with them on a regularly scheduled basis or just call them when you have a specific issue. This can be helpful if you are dealing with important client issues, office politics or career development topics.

Many people turn to family members such as a parent or grandparent for mentorship. This is an ideal situation if that person has achieved the type of success that you desire, as the commitment of a family member to your well-being is unparalleled. Linda has modeled her career after her grandfather, who was not only an award-winning architect but also an extremely good man. She will achieve more in her life because of this relationship.

Regardless of where you find a mentor, having one can help you stay focused on your career goals. A mentor helps you read the maps in that hypothetical cross-country drive. They help you navigate the rough stretches because they have been there before. A good mentor is someone that looks upon your problems as minor pitfalls. Try to find a mentor who is several steps ahead of you in your career. If you are a sales person with just a few years of experience under your belt, look for a Sales VP. Look as far up as you can see and pick that person.

> *"It's important to pick the right role models. You're not looking for people who entertain you or who make you feel good. You're looking for people who can help you."* [9]
>
> —*Rick Pitino*

Do you remember Ebenezer Scrooge, who was rich and successful, but would never help out anyone else? Fortunately he's the exception and not the rule. If you are skilled at building relationships and you are a person of good character, the odds are that you already have been mentored in some manner.

---

9 Rick Pitino, *Success Is A Choice* (Broadway Books, 1997), page 159

Examples of mentors

Deb is a woman in a male-dominated field. During the years she was finishing up her PhD in computational science, she casually mentored many women. Deb also mentored women at The Mathematics and Computer Science division at Argonne National Laboratory, where she worked after she completed her degree.

By far the greatest influence in Mark's career was his first sales manager, Frank. Frank had a straightforward, no-nonsense approach to sales and to cultivating the young sales professionals who worked for him. He taught Mark how to be tenacious in making cold calls. He showed him by example to continue to make call after call, and that the reward would be the achievement of his sales goals. Professionally, Mark could look to Frank as a role model.

Neeracha participated in a formal mentoring program through the Stanford Graduate School of Business. She and Arthur met every few months while she pursued her advanced degree. Following her graduation, they stayed in touch and became good friends, in spite of their 50-year age difference and the fact that he had mentored several dozen students.

Finding a mentor

If you want a formal mentoring relationship then you need to give some advance thought to the details of what such an arrangement involves. You may also have some concerns about selecting the right person, especially if you do not have an ideal candidate in mind.

First, identify the characteristics that your ideal mentor will have:

1. Should they have a specific type of business or industry experience?

2. How old do you think this person should be?

3. Does their gender matter?

4. What do you really expect them to provide for you?

5. Is their physical location an issue?

Second, brainstorm for a list of people who meet these requirements. This is harder. Ask others to make recommendations.

Third, ask them to be your mentor. You may not even need to ask. In some instances you will know it has happened long after the need to ask has passed: you have developed an honest connection with another person. If you have made building a network of relationships a priority, over time you train yourself to recognize these bonds as they first begin to grow. If you are really interested in other people and have their best interest at heart, such relationships will naturally emerge.

If you do need to formally ask, try to have someone find out if they would be receptive to a mentoring role. Once you know that the other person understands mentoring and they are willing to discuss the idea with you, simply call to set up an initial meeting where you can both be honest about how you see such a relationship developing, the time commitment involved and the length of time you will participate. Having specific objectives and accountability will help you both stay focused on the goals of the relationship. You will also want to mutually agree upon strict confidentiality, as both of you will want to feel at ease to share personal and business information with one another. Agree to a set amount of time, perhaps one year, with scheduled meetings every other month. This gives you time to get to know each other and at the end of that time you can decide whether to continue in a structured relationship or move to an informal basis. If you do a good job of building a mutually beneficial friendship, there will be little need to discuss the ongoing relationship, as it will naturally evolve into its own comfort zone.

Be a mentor

As you advance in your career and achieve higher levels of success, you will have the opportunity to mentor others who are coming along behind you. While your path was most likely made easier by those who mentored you, you should take the time to be a mentor to others. Pay it forward. Mentoring can be very rewarding and is not as time consuming as you might think. Being available to share your experiences and seasoned advice with another person will not only make you feel good, but will allow you to grow and learn as well.

Someone may approach you, or you might find them. Either way, they have to be open to listening to your suggestions in order for the relationship to be mutually beneficial. Trust is an integral part of a mentor relationship. As a mentor you can impact them in many ways. Sharing your mistakes can help them avoid tripping up. Your positive examples can assist them in making smart choices, which can allow them a more direct path to success. Additionally, you can open up your network and introduce them to others who can present them with opportunities.

If you had a mentor, or even if you did not, you should find a way to be a mentor. Giving of yourself is very rewarding. It can also benefit you directly because as your mentee advances in his or her career and expands their own network, they will be in a position to return the favor and assist you.

What exactly *is* a Peer Group?

Complementing a mentor relationship or existing on its own is a Peer Group. In a nutshell, a Peer Group is made up of people at similar places in their careers that come together and act as a personal advisory board to each other. For those moving into new career territory, having others that you can turn to for advice and support makes the journey easier and less lonely. Many entrepreneurs use this model of meeting with other entrepreneurs to share best practices. Ideally it becomes an open and safe environment to test business ideas. These groups can be informal gatherings that are put together by the entrepreneurs themselves, or a more formal group with dues and bylaws. In some cities the local Chamber of Commerce organizes formal groups for business owners to meet with other like-minded business owners. The Young Entrepreneur's Organization also does this.

One Peer Group

During the year I turned 30, I started to notice that some people were pulling ahead of others, career-wise. I wanted to get ahead, but was unsure exactly how to do it. Two friends and I discussed forming a group with whom we could, over time, develop a trusting and mutually beneficial relationship.

There were seven of us: four men and three women, all from non-competitive industries. We were either in sales or were small business owners. We agreed to meet twice a month, once for breakfast, the other for happy hour, with a one-year commitment. At the end of that year we would evaluate the group's effectiveness.

Our first few gatherings were spent getting to know each other and developing ground rules. With seven energetic individuals, it took little time for us to become fast friends. Over the next year we took turns sharing our ambitions and career pitfalls. Others in the group could chime in and make recommendations, and/or make introductions to others in our networks that could be of assistance. In time we came to see each other as shoulders to lean on, sounding boards and advisors. The group was made up of a diverse group of professionals with different perspectives and unique views of business interactions. Everyone had different educational and economic backgrounds. While each person had extensive local contacts, those contacts were not from the same industries.

After a year, we all agreed that the group was instrumental in our career growth. Three members of the group had successfully surpassed sales quotas, one made partner in her firm, another started his own businesses, and another found new, better employment.

During the second year three members dropped out because of life changes. But the four remaining members kept the group going. Many things happened in our lives, personally and professionally during this time; we shared successes and failures. Yet each of us will tell you that we were better off because of the group than we ever would have been on our own. While we are no longer a formal peer group, we are still close friends.

"We all know that two heads are better than one when it comes to solving a problem or creating a result. Imagine having a permanent group of five to six people who meet every week for the purpose of problem solving, brainstorming, networking and encouraging and motivating each other. I don't know anybody who has become super successful who has not employed the principle of masterminding." [10]

—*Jack Canfield*

Organizing your own Peer Group

Finding the people to be part of a proactive peer group is similar to finding a mentor. While some people may be obvious, it's important to include people who are not already your friends.

Start with one or two people you already know and respect who are committed to growing their network and advancing their career. While it's not crucial to keep the group's existence a secret, it's advisable because it prevents others from asking to join. Once the group begins meeting it's hard to add people because of the amount of time that is invested early on building trust amongst the participants.

---

10 Jack Canfield, *The Success Principles* (HarperResource, 2004), page 307

Once you have one or two others, each of you should look at your own list of contacts and add one or two more. Limit this to between five and eight people total. This allows for some attrition, and the group remains small enough where everyone can really get to know each other.

Set ground rules early. If someone's work schedule is irregular and does not allow them to make most meetings, find someone else. Like a mentor relationship, confidentiality is a must. Discuss this at your first meeting and get buy off on the rules and structure. Be sure that everyone gets a chance to talk about themselves at the first few meetings. In the future it is a good idea to rotate, letting each member and his or her issues be the center of attention.

For the group to succeed, everyone must make attending and participating a priority. Keep in mind that even with a successful group of people who develop close relationships, the group will eventually play itself out. And that's okay. It served its purpose.

The Long Haul

A mentor or a peer group will not be able to influence your career by itself. Mentors and peers do not serve the same purpose as your mother; they will not hold your hand and look out for you every time you reach an intersection.

It takes more than just hanging the title of mentor or peer group member around someone's neck to make the relationship flourish.

You will be disappointed if you are expecting the real benefits of a mentor or peer group relationship to be visible in a month. No one is going to go out of his or her way for you until you have proven yourself first.

Most people you meet will want to see you succeed. The trick is being able to identify the difference. If you have a long-term focus, and so do your mentors and peers, then you will see rewards.

Take Aways:

1. *A mentor has already achieved what you wish to achieve and is committed to helping you.*

2. *A peer group is your personal career advisory board.*

3. *People want to help you and will also benefit from the relationship.*

10

PERFECTING YOUR CRAFT:

NEVER STOP LEARNING

Although you may no longer be enrolled in school, you should continue your education. No matter what your profession, there are always new discoveries and best practices. In addition, to maintain your value add with others in your network you need to keep up with current events and other trends. With the amount of information available today, no one person could ever keep up with everything. There are many ways to develop your new skills, and you should not just limit yourself to one type of learning. Embrace knowledge and continue to explore.

Read. Then Read Some More.

Keeping abreast of current events is one of the best things a person can do to help advance their career. It is essential to building a wide and diverse network. If you believe in just some of the things in this book then you know that it's key to be interested in things that are of interest to other people. While knowledge of pop culture, television and celebrity gossip is important, it will only get you so far. A balance of media is best.

Finding the time to be well read is often a challenge for most people. Like anything, if you make it a regular part of your schedule, make it a priority, it will become easier to accomplish.

Try leaving for work thirty minutes early every day; this way you can avoid the traffic and sit in a coffee shop en route to catch up on your reading. By spending that time on reading, you can keep up on current events and finish more books. Read books some days, magazines on others.

Thom's System:
I try to digest a "BLT" every day. I make it a goal to learn something new about Business on a national or international level, something new Locally to my geography, and something new Topically related to my particular area of expertise. This method helps me balance my knowledge and not focus on one area more than another since I need to know about all three to be successful.

Newspapers

There is no excuse for not at least skimming the headlines in your local paper every day.

I'm like you. I don't have time to read the paper every day. I do, however, flip through both our local paper and the *Wall Street Journal*. This can take as little as ten minutes or as long as an hour depending on the amount of time I have. The headline and photos can give you enough information to get by if the subject should come up in conversation. Even if you are not a big sports fan, it is still important to keep up with major sporting news, such as knowing that Tiger Woods just won another Masters. Knowing what is happening in the national business community helps you spot trends locally.

Internet News Sites

Complementing or replacing the traditional print media are online news sites. Most news media have websites that follow the top stories of the day, and there are thousands of other sites that also have local, national and international news. While you need to be careful about the slant and sources for your online news, just as you do with other media sources, it is an efficient way to keep up with breaking news or specialty information. Identify relevant websites and newsletters, and either bookmark them or use RSS technology to subscribe to updates to them. Electronic media also has the advantage of being searchable, something that cannot be done with a newspaper you have already recycled.

Magazines

Many periodicals cover national and world news. Many business magazines are monthlies, so they can be read from cover to cover. Newsweeklies such as *TIME* and *Newsweek* are a little harder to work into a busy schedule.

Thom's System:
When I just don't have time to read my newsweekly, my wife helps: she reads these magazines, too, and flags articles she thinks I should read. When all else fails I just throw the back copies away and start fresh.

There are thousands of business publications out there. Select two that best satisfy your job focus and industry. Read them religiously.

Finally, when you are at the dentist's office, sneak a peak at *People* or one of the other magazines that cover celebrities and pop culture. You can subscribe or buy an occasional issue, but it's likely that this, coupled with the other things you read, will provide you with all you need to know about the rich and famous to make conversation on it.

Books

Read the bestsellers. Read business books. Read autobiographies. Read the classics if you have not already done so. Read books that interest you.

The busiest and most successful people, the ones who are doing amazing things in their careers and who are active in their family lives, still find time to read. Reading is learning. Read while on the treadmill. Read while taking public transit to work. Keep a book or magazine with you so that if you arrive early at an appointment or someone keeps you waiting you can make use of that time. Cut back on the amount of television you watch or the hours you spend online. According to the Jenkins Group, an independent publishing services firm, 42% of college graduates never read another book." Set a good example for your kids; make reading a priority.

Thom's System:
I am always looking for great business books and biographies to read. When I get a suggestion from someone in my network, hear about a title on NPR or read a favorable book review on a topic that interests me, I add it to a list I keep on my PDA. By always having this list with me, I never forget to add a book of interest. It also comes in handy when I am stuck in an airport with nothing new read; I just check my list and pop into the airport bookstore to make a purchase. It also is great to have on hand when the kids are running loose in Barnes & Noble on the weekends...I can dash over to the business section. Knowing which books you want to read saves you a lot of time browsing around the aisles.

Blogs

If you spend any time at all on the Internet then you know that blogs have become a major communication medium. Regardless of your industry, somebody somewhere authors a blog about topics that can be valuable to you and your career. A blog, or weblog, is an informal online tool for people to share their ideas, thoughts, tips, and points of view. While there are countless blogs out there, a simple Google search can help you find a few that will be of interest to you. Most successful bloggers regularly add informative articles and links to other sources.

In addition to reading blogs, you may want to consider writing your own. A blog is easy to start and there are many free online services, like Blogger.com, that allow you to begin blogging. There are many reasons why writing a blog is a good idea. First, it will help you fine tune your writing skills; creating a 200 to 600 word post three to five days a week will force you to tighten you mastery of the written word. Second, you will find yourself analyzing everything you read in your area of expertise in order to develop clarified thoughts on how to express your own opinion on the topic on your blog. Third, blogging is a great networking tool as you will start to develop friendships with other bloggers who cover the same topics. And finally, having a blog is a great way to develop material for writing articles or books for future publication. You can take your blog posts and re-write and re-position them in other mediums, and help expand your personal brand.

Conferences and Seminars

In your quest to further your professional education, making the time to attend conferences and seminars is a smart idea. In addition to the networking opportunities that exist at industry conferences, there are many educational opportunities that can help you keep ahead of the competition. Sessions are often led by industry experts or important vendors with productivity enhancing products. While many conferences have a cost associated with them and may involve travel, the good ones are always worth the time and money. In addition, there are many local single-day seminars which provide an intensive way to keep your skill set more than just current.

People often do not participate in conferences claiming that they cannot be out of the office for any period of time, or that they do not believe that these events provide enough information. Frankly, the former is just an excuse for people who are uncomfortable with the networking aspect that goes along with conference attendance. As for the latter objection about the curriculum, any time you can be in a room full of people with similar careers and interests, you should find a way to be there. You never know whom you might meet.

Still, you must do more than show up; you need to make an effort to meet other people. Use the non-classroom time to your benefit; networking can be done at lunch, dinner and on coffee breaks. Is there a bar in the hotel lobby? Often that is a good place to meet people.

When budgets are tight it often takes a little effort to convince your boss that taking the time and money to attend a seminar is in the best interest of the company. Make it a habit of always writing a short report for your co-workers on what you learned at a conference and whom you met. Some people falsely think that seminars and conferences are just an excuse to get out of the office and party. You need to demonstrate to those around you that these types of events can be very beneficial to your co-workers and the company itself. If you always do a great job of meeting new contacts and finding new business, there will be no problem with your participation.

Local Universities and Colleges

Most local colleges offer continuing education programs for professionals. Some are even accompanied by a certification. In addition, these programs may provide opportunities to meet successful, key individuals in the local business community who serve as adjunct professors to teach these courses or come in as guest lecturers. Active participation in the class is a great way to establish a rapport with the instructor, which may translate into a future business friendship.

Volunteering

The more involved you become with others in your network, the more opportunities you will discover to serve on boards or donate your time for worthy causes. These types of activities can be very useful tools in building relationships and are also a great way to learn new skills.

If there are charities whose missions are near and dear to you, by all means volunteer. Helping others is a great way to relax and feel more connected to your community. Volunteering will expose you to a variety of people from different ethnic and socio-economic backgrounds. By working alongside people you may not encounter during your day job, you will be exposed to other points of view and have opportunities to learn about things that had previously not even occurred to you.

Serving on Boards

It is very common for executives to volunteer their expertise for organizations that promote a cause. By being active with these organizations and serving in a leadership capacity, you will not only meet these important people, but also work closely with them on projects. The tasks that you will undertake in this capacity often will be things that you may not do in your daily job. If you are not a CPA, but assist with an organization's finances, this will give you the chance to upgrade your bookkeeping skills. If you are not in sales, but you take on a fundraising role, you will learn how to make cold calls. A board of any type has a variety of leadership positions where you can stretch out of your comfort zone. Having tackled these jobs will keep you learning and enhance your resumé.

Be Inquisitive

Meetings or presentations typically end the same way: the speaker asks the audience if there are any questions. The majority of the people in the room just sit there and stare at their shoes. For some reason, people do not ask questions, even in a situation where they are solicited. If people are not asking questions when asked, it follows that they are not asking them at other times either.

Seek first to understand

Asking is a great way to interactively learn more about a subject or person. Aim for open-ended questions. By learning how other people view the world, you can gain a different perspective and also gather insight into that individual's personality.

One reason people do not ask questions is that they fear they will appear uninformed. When you are engaged in a conversation and do not fully grasp what the other person is saying, probe deeper. When the person you are talking with realizes that you are interested in what they have to say, they will happily tell you more. Most people find a person who inquires to be very intelligent.

Request feedback

Ask those in your network how you can improve in your business and community involvement. People rarely solicit feedback.

An employee might have an annual review. Few managers or employees look forward to this exercise. It often gets glossed over and sugar coated to make it just end. Yet this is a great chance to really learn how you are perceived. Such feedback does not have to only come from your superiors. You can also ask your co-workers, clients, and those in your network to help you discover how you can improve. This can easily take place informally. Think water cooler chit chat.

Ask to learn

You can ask someone for their point of view or advice on how you can learn more. My friend Kevin is a NASCAR fanatic and has what some consider to be a fantasy job—he manages his company's promotions at weekly NASCAR events. When I want to learn more about product promotion at racing events, I go to lunch with him. Since he attends dozens of races each year and has for the last several years, he always has insightful thoughts that help me strengthen my own product positioning.

If you ask people questions that they know the answers to, they will usually talk. People like to talk and they appreciate it when others seek out their advice.

Smart people continuously seek knowledge. Try to learn something new every single day. The people in your network and those you encounter on a daily basis can all be great teachers. Make it your goal to walk away from each personal interaction with just a little more knowledge than you had before.

Take Aways:

1. *Make it a daily habit to read a book, newspaper or other media.*

2. *Ask questions, and listen to the answers.*

3. *Seek knowledge on a variety of subjects and about different types of people.*

11

THE FINISHING TOUCHES:

TURNING YOUR NETWORK

INTO REAL BUSINESS

It's much easier to build a network than it is to actually ask those you know for business. Some people work hard to build capital with others, yet never ask them for help. Just like building strong business relationships is a learned skill, so is calling upon others to help you. If you are a sales veteran, chances are that you are already good at this. If you're not, with practice you will learn to turn your network and your investment in helping others into real dollars.

Getting the Business

People who are skeptical about the importance of having a network often ask if you really can get business from networking. Results vary, of course, depending on the individual and their field of expertise.

Building relationships exposes you to opportunities. People often wonder if it is okay for salespeople to ask for referrals from their clients, or if it would be perceived as pushy. If you have no real relationship, it's not only pushy but inappropriate as well. However, if you have a real friendship with your client then it is simply expected. So expected that it will most likely be seamless.

People who claim that others do not ever give them referrals should examine how they are treating others. If you have a large network and no one is helping you then it's not a network. You may know a lot of people by name but you have not succeeded in building true relationships. The people who whine that they never get anything from networking are usually the people who are just trying to take.

Are there times when you need to ask people you know for their business or for a referral? Absolutely, because even when it is happening all around you automatically, certain individuals just need to be asked. Some people just feel awkward about this. If you have invested enough in the relationship, it should not be uncomfortable to ask this of a friend.

If you have given referrals to the other person, and demonstrated time after time that you have their best interests at heart, then you should have no problem turning your connection with them into business referrals.

Build Internal Support by Sharing your Network

Your network also extends into your employer. There are many advantages to being seen as a resource by your co-workers. Find ways to build your internal network, and allow those in your company to reach out to your external network. Done correctly, this can be good for the individuals you work with and for the company. However, you have to be careful because, while you can pick the people you network with in the outside world and thus avoid takers and all-around bad eggs, you cannot choose your co-workers.

Your internal network will include individuals whom you know do not have your best interests at heart, but whom you must deal with regularly. While there is no way to avoid office politics, you can stay out of the middle of it and try not to be brought down by it.

Using your network to avoid office politics

If you bring the same dedication to helping others to your internal marketing, you can avoid most of the office politics. People rarely badmouth or gossip about people they know can help them out later.

When you have a large network of contacts, be careful to not appear like you are just out on the cocktail party circuit. People who do not understand networking will often think that attending seminars, giving speeches and writing articles is not work-related. Done properly, it is part of a long-term career strategy to get more business and better career opportunities. Since you have the interest of getting more business for your company as a major reason for building your network, bring your co-workers along and help them make some connections. Introduce your co-workers to people in your network because you have a responsibility to your company. If you do leave later, you will have done a good job of cultivating those relationships and the business will follow. If you do a bad job, then the business will stay with those who did a better job. In the end, if you are not confident enough in your relationships with your contacts, then you are at risk of losing the business anyway.

Taking this a step further, one of the smartest things you can do is to introduce your higher ups to those in your network. Many of them already have lists of people they have developed solid friendships with over the years but no one smart in business is opposed to meeting other key people. If you know someone that your manager could benefit from knowing, or if your companies could do business together, facilitate the introduction. If you can help your manager meet some peers or other beneficial VIPs in your local community, then you will be viewed as an important company resource. Important resources retain their jobs during downsizing.

Never Burn a Bridge

How you say goodbye is just as important as how you say hello. When you decide to leave a company, a board on which you serve or another organization, consider your relationships with the people there. The reason for your departure may be positive, in which case it is easy to remain on good terms. This is the case when those you leave behind can clearly see that it is in your best interest and does not negatively impact their lives. Conversely, you might be severing your association ties because of negative reasons. You could be leaving to join a competitor or leaving a volunteer position mid-term because of other obligations. If your departure will create challenges for those you leave behind, you need to be extra cautious of what you say and how you treat the others.

Joining a competitor

People who join a competitor almost always try to take clients with them. This can set up some ill will by your former co-workers. They might feel threatened by your departure, and it may cause them added stress. Tread very cautiously with what you say to those former co-workers and to others in the community about the company you left behind. People who leave one company and directly or indirectly condemn their former employer and co-workers hope that this will make them stand out to clients and prospects as they now focus on building their business at a new company. The problem with this is that it is never in your best interest to say anything negative. Often enough, things one says are repeated to those one says them about. If you put it in an email, you can be sure that it will be forwarded to the people you are addressing.

There are many good reasons to leave a job and join a competitor. The best way the way to do this is to simply tell people that it's a better opportunity and focus on the strengths of the new company.

Volunteer positions

The same is true if you leave a volunteer organization. Many people abandon their commitments to a board on which they serve. The others with whom your responsibilities are shifted will not appreciate your departure, especially if you are negative about the organization or nonchalant about your departure. If you have to leave a volunteer position before you have completed your term, and this can happen for a variety of legitimate reasons, be very supportive of the organization. If appropriate, try to find others from your company or network who can step in and complete your obligation. Even if the organization is not your highest priority, it is important to others. If you belittle the commitment to the organization, you are belittling those who dedicate their resources to it.

Beware the Boomerang Effect

How you depart will stay in the minds and hearts of those you leave behind. One never knows when your paths will cross again. Rob left his job because he did not like his manager. He joined a lesser-known competitor. While he did not burn his bridges and bad-mouth the boss in his exit interview, he was not shy about his disdain for his boss to others in the community. Three years later the two companies merged and he got his old boss back.

Take Aways:

1. *If you do a good job of building relationships, you will not have to ask people to assist you in advancing your business.*

2. *Your network is not just an asset for you, it is also an asset to your employer. Make sure your employer knows this.*

3. *Depart graciously.*

CONCLUSION

Making Networking Work For You

People with large, functional networks understand that other people are a valuable resource. Like money in the bank that is both saved for a rainy day and pays interest, your network is important for both today's business and as an investment in your future. Seasoned networkers enjoy finding ways to assist others; they like to connect people and watch the results.

Career-long employment by the same company is no longer reality. In the private sector, no substitutes exist for hard work. New technologies cannot build your relationships nor can you delegate the responsibility of relationship cultivation to anyone else. Skilled networking makes good professionals great. Savvy networking is something that is both natural and transparent. It just comes across as being friendly and interested in those around you. While it doesn't come easily to everyone, it can be learned using the basics in this book.

The results will not happen overnight, and you will not necessarily know when and where the payoff will occur. Building a network of professional contacts and cultivating those contacts into long-term business or personal friendships is a never-ending adventure. The best networkers and the most successful ones will keep at it and have fun along the way.

RECOMMENDED READING

Becoming a Category of One: How Extraordinary Companies Transcend Commodity and Defy Comparison, Joe Calloway (Wiley, 2003)

The 7 Habits of Highly Effective People: Powerful Lessons in Personal Change, Stephen R. Covey (Free Press, 2004)

Good to Great: Why Some Companies Make the Leap ... and Others Don't, Jim Collins (HarperBusiness, 2001)

What Clients Love: A Field Guide to Growing Your Business, Harry Beckwith (Warner Business Books, 2003)

Dig Your Well before You're Thirsty: The only networking book you'll ever need, Harvey B. Mackay (Currency, 1999)

Sharkproof: Get the Job You Want, Keep the Job You Love ... in Today's Frenzied Job Market, Harvey B. Mackay (Harper Collins, 1994)

Control Your Destiny or Someone Else Will, Noel M. Tichy, Stratford Sherman (HarperBusiness, 2001)

Love Is the Killer App: How to Win Business and Influence Friends, Tim Sanders (Crown Business, 2002)

Now, Discover Your Strengths, Marcus Buckingham, Donald O. Clifton (Free Press, 2001)

Man's Search for Meaning, Viktor E. Frankl (Pocket, 1997)

Self-Made in America: Plain Talk for Plain People About the Meaning of Success, John McCormack (Addison Wesley, 1992)

Peak Performers: The New Heroes of American Business, Charles A. Garfield (Quill, 1991)

The Road Less Traveled, 25th Anniversary Edition: A New Psychology of Love, Traditional Values and Spiritual Growth, M. Scott Peck (Touchstone, 2003)

How to Win Friends & Influence People, Dale Carnegie (Pocket, 1990)

The Power of Positive Thinking, Norman Vincent Peale (Ballantine Books, 1996)

The Greatest Salesman in the World, Og Mandino (Bantam, 1983)

Think and Grow Rich, Napoleon Hill, Ross Cornwell (Avantine Press, 2004)

Customers For Life: How To Turn That One-Time Buyer Into a Lifetime Customer, Carl Sewell, Paul B. Brown (Currency, 2002)

Over The Top, Zig Ziglar (Nelson Books, 1997)

Success Is a Choice: Ten Steps to Overachieving in Business and Life, Rick Pitino (Broadway, 1998)

Awaken the Giant Within: How to Take Immediate Control of Your Mental, Emotional, Physical, and Financial Destiny, Anthony Robbins (Free Press, 1992)

The Success Principles, Jack Canfield (Collins, 2004)

Freakonomics, Steven Levitt (William Morrow, 2006)

Often Wrong, Never in Doubt, Donny Deutsch (Collins, 2005)

The Art of Acting, Stella Adler (Applause Book, 2000)

Talent Is Never Enough, John Maxwell (Nelson Business, 2007)

Selling To Big Companies, Jill Konrath (Kaplan Business, 2005)

It's Called WORK for a Reason, Larry Wignet (Gotham, 2006)

The Ripple Effect, Steve Harper (SWOT Publishing, 2005)

ABOUT THE AUTHOR

Thom Singer has nearly two decades of marketing and business development experience with firms such as RR Donnelley, Brobeck Phleger & Harrison LLP, Andrews Kurth LLP, Marsh, Inc., and Wells Fargo Bank. He is an expert in branding, positioning and networking, and has trained more than 2,000 professionals in the art of building professional contacts that lead to increased business.

Thom has authored numerous articles for business and marketing publications, including The Austin Business Journal, The Legal Marketing Portal and Professional Marketers Forum Magazine. An accomplished speaker and presenter, Thom was a semi-finalist in the 2002 Toastmasters International World Championship of Public Speaking, placing second in the Region III competition, making him among the top 20 Toastmasters of 20,000 who competed that year. He is also the creator of the online networking skills assessment tool, The Networking Quotient (www.qquiz.com)

Thom and his wife, Sara, make their home in Austin, Texas and are the parents of two daughters.

He can be emailed at thom@thomsinger.com.

ORDER FORM

Fax orders: Fax this form to 425-984-7256.

Telephone orders: Call 925-838-9806.

Please have your credit card ready.

Email orders: orders@newyearpublishing.com

Postal orders by credit card or personal check:

> *New Year Publishing, LLC*
> *PO Box 12793*
> *Austin, TX 78711 USA*

I would like additional information on:

_____Speaking _____Seminars _____ Consulting

Name:_____

Address: _____

City: _____ State: _____ Zip: _____

Telephone: _____

Email: _____

_____ Quantity @ $21.95 for *Some Assembly Required*

_____ Quantity @ $29.95 for two books: *Some Assembly Required* and *The ABC's of Networking*

Bulk discounts are available. Call New Year Publishing for additional information.

Sales tax: Please add 8.25% for books shipped to California.

Shipping: $5.95 per book.

_____ **Total including applicable tax and shipping**

Payment: ____ Check ____ Credit card

Card number: _____

Name on card:_____

Exp. date:_____